Programming: A Primer

Coding for Beginners

ICP Primers in Electronics and Computer Science (ICPPECS)

ISSN: 2054-4537

Series Editor: Mark S. Nixon *(University of Southampton, UK)*

Published

Vol. 1 Digital Electronics: A Primer
Introductory Logic Circuit Design
by Mark S. Nixon

Vol. 2 Programming: A Primer
Coding for Beginners
by Tom Bell

ICP Primers in Electronics and Computer Science Vol. 2

Programming: A Primer

Coding for Beginners

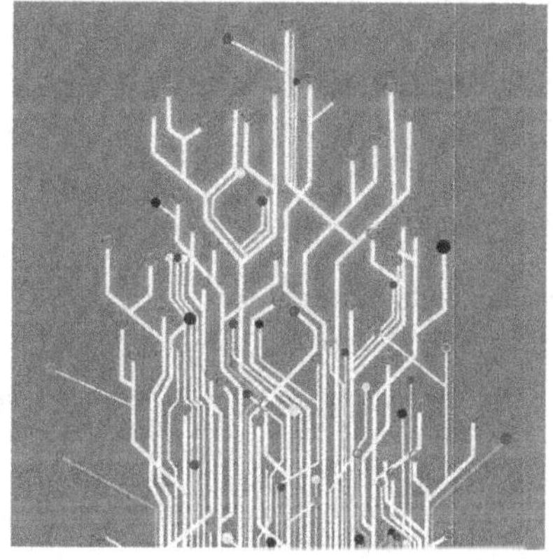

Tom Bell
University of Southampton, UK

ICP Imperial College Press

Published by

Imperial College Press
57 Shelton Street
Covent Garden
London WC2H 9HE

Distributed by

World Scientific Publishing Co. Pte. Ltd.

5 Toh Tuck Link, Singapore 596224

USA office: 27 Warren Street, Suite 401-402, Hackensack, NJ 07601

UK office: 57 Shelton Street, Covent Garden, London WC2H 9HE

Library of Congress Cataloging-in-Publication Data
Bell, Tom (Electronic engineer)
Programming : a primer coding for beginners / by Tom Bell (University of Southampton, UK).
pages cm -- (ICP primers in electronics and computer science)
Includes bibliographical references and index.
ISBN 978-1-78326-706-4 (alk. paper) -- ISBN 978-1-78326-707-1 (alk. paper)
1. Computer programming. 2. Microcomputers--Programming. I. Title.
QA76.6.B4367 2015
005.1--dc23

2015011283

British Library Cataloguing-in-Publication Data
A catalogue record for this book is available from the British Library.

In-house Editors: Thomas Stottor/Dipasri Sardar

Typeset by Stallion Press
Email: enquires@stallionpress.com

Printed in Singapore

"Anyone who stops learning is old, whether at twenty or eighty. Anyone who keeps learning stays young."

Henry Ford
Founder of Ford Motoring Company

To my friends and family

Acknowledgements

Many thanks to all the people who have helped me write this book. First, to Jasmine Brown and James Sharkey who have spent countless hours before publication reading drafts and refining them. They have given their time and effort to proofreading this book, and their kindness is hugely appreciated.

Secondly, to Jenna Watt, Hollie James, James Patterson, Gareth Clarridge — and my father Steve Bell — who have supported me in filtering the content for clarity and helpfulness, and their contributions are much appreciated.

Thirdly, to my parents, who have taught me to value work highly and to help others in what I do. My family have been incredible examples to me of people who serve each other and the local community through practical love and hospitality.

Finally, to my friends at Christ Church Southampton who supported me throughout the many months I spent writing. They encouraged me to work diligently and have been a joy to know, love and grow with over the past few years.

Contents

Read Me First

Over the past few decades, computers have radically changed the way we run our lives. They have affected the availability of information, our methods of communication with friends and family, education, business, healthcare and our study of the universe. With the availability of technology and the immense power at the fingertips of anyone who can use it, programming literacy has become one of the most sought-after skills on the planet.

Only recently has computer science become a core aspect of the school curriculum. This is great news for children and young people, but what about those who've already finished those stages in life? What about those who've missed the boat? To the vast majority of us who fall into this category, it's our task to begin the journey of gaining a functional understanding of programming, while acquiring the confidence and commitment to put our ideas into code.

I still remember how I began my journey. A few simple searches on Google during my time at high school, such as "How to program", "How do I become an iOS developer?" or "How to be Mark Zuckerberg". It was the same place that it starts for many programmers, and it's a legitimate place to start. Search for "Learning to code in C" and you'll find some well-written online tutorials, or for "Which programming language should I learn first?" and you'll find some critical and interesting articles comparing JavaScript with Python as a starting point. This form of learning is great for answering those specific questions you have as a beginner, but it lacks something essential — it won't teach you the broader context or the technical framework into which findings from your own learning will fit. If you pick up a hefty 500-page textbook on Python for beginners, it will teach you Python, but it won't make you an agile programmer, able to adapt quickly to solve new problems.

An alternative to this self-study approach is to undertake some kind of formal education in programming. Study Computer Science at degree level, or go to college to study Software Development. These can be fantastic courses, and I greatly valued my time at university, but this option is not available to many of us. With jobs, families, and/or financial constraints it can be impossible to spend three years learning to code. Or maybe you're at university already, but you chose a different degree and are already half way through a course in Geography or Fine Arts. Besides, a degree isn't by any means necessary for equipping you to solve the vast majority of programming challenges out there — in fact, you're free and able to do it yourself, just as you are.

Programming: A Primer addresses this situation. In writing this book, my goal is to inspire you, and to help you harness your urge to invent, to build and to circulate your own ideas, through teaching you the fundamental concepts behind modern programming. I want to help you understand the powerful tools at your disposal, and to offer you a glimpse at the vast ocean of possibilities for changing the world for the better though programming. My assumption, therefore, is that your approach is practical, not academic and that you actually want yourself or others to benefit in some way from what you'll able to do. So if you're approaching coding with a "cut out the nonsense and tell me only what I need to know" outlook, you've got the right book.

This is primarily an introduction to the fundamental concepts in computer programming and not a step-by-step tutorial for simply learning a particular programming language. As such there won't be detailed instructions on what to do in order to get your development environment set up on a range of platforms, nor will there be a comprehensive coverage of all the features of the relevant programming languages. On the contrary, this book is a journey from alienation to familiarity with the ideas behind programming. You'll be introduced to the basic concepts of various programming languages, so that you can go away and learn a few for yourself with ease. You'll find out about what the different languages are used for, and how to write powerful programs quickly. Languages for designing powerful websites will be introduced. Database languages, and a selection of popular algorithms will be explained. In later chapters, we'll take a look at where technology is heading, and how developers can benefit.

The reality about being a programmer is that it's not a job title, or an honorary title given for graduating with a technical degree. It's primarily a mind-set, which uses the power of computing to solve new and interesting problems. Programmers can be

- Student entrepreneurs designing the next social network.
- Accountants seeking more efficient ways to manage clients' book-keeping.
- Professionals who want to help make law, medicine or science more interesting and accessible.
- Long-term unemployed adults looking to make the most of their time.
- Social entrepreneurs providing content management systems for charities, churches and other causes.

Teachers, doctors, engineers or builders are all one and the same when it comes to programming — they are problem solvers. The key to success in problem solving is in familiarity with the principles, being aware of the tools and dreaming up the possibilities.

To get the most out of this journey, I would recommend skim reading each chapter first, and then going over them much more slowly; digesting all the new ideas and knowledge, and fitting the pieces together.

With all of this in mind, let us get going!

Starting Point

Chapter 1

Introduction

For many of us, computer programming is an unwelcome thought. The phrase rings alarm bells, conjuring up ideas of tedious typing, complex concepts and mind-bending mathematics that are difficult to understand or engage with. These preconceptions can stand between us and one of the greatest tools for progress that humankind has at its disposal. As I hope to show, the reality of programming is different. Programming is an instrument that can be learned by any patient and determined novice who is open to creating within themselves a new talent. You do not need to spend years learning how a computer works from the ground up before you can reach competency in writing software. A skilled craftsman does not need to know how his machinery was built in order to be able to create something with it. For computer programmers, programming is a tool for making their ideas a reality.

What is Programming?

Programming is the process of specifying a set of instructions to be performed by a computer in order to solve a problem. Programmers use a 'programming language' to instruct a computer how to behave. Programming languages are a vocabulary and set of grammatical rules for instructing a computer to perform specific tasks. Each language has a set of keywords and a special syntax for organising computer instructions. These languages are intended to be 'human readable', so people can write programs with them, and modify the programmes in accordance with their requirements.

Why Learn to Program?

So why take the time to learn how to program? It is probably the first question you have, and it's a fair one. As I hope to show, there are a good number of reasons why you should learn to program. I will take you through some of the most significant.

First, business and social enterprises are started when a problem is identified, and a solution is sought. Microsoft and Apple saw the problems involved with manual data storage, computation and communication, and so developed personal computers. Facebook identified a range of problems associated with poor connections between individuals across the world and created the social media platform we use today. LinkedIn was born in 2003 when Reid Hoffman *et al.* sought to put our business networking online in order to solve problems regarding finding talent, managing business connections and presenting one's professional credentials to potential employers. These are the big household names of the technology industry, but every year tens of thousands of entrepreneurs solve problems, create businesses and change the world through delivering new websites, apps and desktop software to the world. Learn to program to *solve big problems.*

Second, computers are in billions of homes, offices and pockets across the globe. They are the devices we use every day, and that's not going to change. If you are a reasonably competent computer programmer you will never find yourself without a job. You can work as a self-employed web developer or a mobile application consultant. You can work for a company in the technology industry or sell your own indie games. In a growing market with a high demand for skilled programmers you'll never be out of a job for long. Learn to program for a *career.*

Third, all of us enjoy doing things that are skilful. We learn to dance, or play the piano, write a journal or spend an afternoon painting a glorious landscape. Many of us enjoy creating, whether it is works of literature or choreography. Programming is a hugely creative challenge. I have enjoyed spending countless hours designing beautiful websites or smartphone apps that have been technically and aesthetically satisfying. That is something which is hugely rewarding. Learn to program for *fun*.

There are a host of other reasons why you should learn to program. There may be a specific project you may have in mind, or you can do it as an intellectual challenge, or even just to show off a new skill to your friends. Whatever your age, parental responsibilities, occupation or intellectual ability, programming is an enjoyable, achievable and practical skill allowing the creation of all sorts of applications for the benefit of you and others.

How does a Program Work?

The primary purpose of the entire engineering enterprise is to find ways of using natural laws to create things that solve problems. Small and simple components are designed from scientific principles, and then combined together to form more complex and powerful parts, that are then assembled to form systems that simplify the execution of complex operations. This concept is known as *abstraction*. A camshaft and crankshaft are simple components, which form part of an engine, which is itself a significant component of a car. A car is a complex object with powerful capabilities, yet it can be used without knowing how it works. Abstracting away complex components 'under the hood' is how we create simple yet powerful tools such as the vehicles we use every day.

Computers are the same. They're made of thousands of components which themselves are multi-part, and which are precisely manufactured to have very specific function. An operating system (OS) such as Windows 8 is an extension of this process. It hides a lot of complex behaviour, so the user can use the computer intuitively and easily. Each layer of complexity in the design of a laptop, for instance, is a layer of abstraction building upon the complexity of the layers before it.

Generally, a computer program is best described as one primary layer of abstraction. It uses the rich features of simple programming languages available to the developer to create a powerful and simple experience for the end user to enjoy. A program, then, is a sequence of instructions run on a computer in order to achieve some task. Websites, apps and enterprise software can all be described as a sequence of instructions to be executed by a computer. Typically, they have some kind of input, some kind of processing capability or functionality and, finally, an output.

To give some examples — a game has input from your joystick or keyboard, performs calculations to process your movements into gameplay, and then outputs the gameplay on screen. An automatic trading agent takes in stock market data, attempts to learn the behaviour of the stock, and, as an output, predicts the stock's future price (to varying degrees of accuracy). Perhaps a bit closer to home, a web browser takes a HTML file as its input, processes it by converting the HTML into a page of text and graphics, and then displays the content.

In each of these examples the programmer, through explicit instructions, dictates the behaviour of the software — 'show this picture', 'calculate this equation', for example. Of course the instructions aren't quite that simple and we need to understand exactly how we can tell the computer what to do, which is what we'll look at for the remainder of this chapter.

Programming Languages

The English language is a language that only humans can understand. Computers are designed to understand a different language. They only respond to 1s and 0s. Every operation of a computer can be reduced to this binary behaviour. The role of a programming language is to act as a crossover language that can be easily read and understood by humans, but can also be translated into 1s and 0s (so called *machine language*) for the computer to understand.

A collection of instructions that achieves some computational goal forms the basis of a program. These instructions need to be understood by a human and translated into machine language. The 'human readable' code is known as *source code*. This is the raw file written by a human in the programming language they are using, which will later be translated and used by the computer.

There are two categories of languages, and their names depict the way in which they are executed on a computer — *compiled* and *interpreted*. Compiled programming languages are those whose source code is first written and later translated into a separate executable file by a *compiler*. The compiler turns the source code into the machine code that can be directly run on the computer. Examples of some popular compiled programming languages include C, C++ ('C-plus-plus') and C# ('C-sharp'). Interpreted languages, such as Python, JavaScript and Ruby, are those for whom the executable file is the same as the source code file. That is, the file containing the source code is executed by an *interpreter*, which translates the source code into executable code at the moment of execution. This removes the need for compiling.

Every programming language has its own benefits and drawbacks for each application. Each language is designed for a specific kind of use and each behaves in a slightly different way. There are general ideas that are shared across different languages, but the behaviour, look and feel of each language is different.

An important characteristic of a programming language, which you will eventually learn to identify when looking at different languages, is the extent to which a language is separated in its behaviour from the underlying behaviour of the processor. This is the concept of *abstraction* that we've already come across — separating functionality or behaviour from the details about how something works.

Programming languages are abstracted from the detail of the binary operations of the computer in machine language to different extents. Each programming language can be placed on a scale from *low-level* languages (low or no level of abstraction from machine language) to *high-level* languages (strong abstraction). Low-level languages such as Assembly, C and C++ are bare-metal languages, which provide low abstraction. Assembler simply translates the binary of machine language into named commands and labels. C and C++ provide more abstraction but are nowadays considered fairly low-level languages. High-level languages include JavaScript, C# and interpreted languages, which are typically easier for humans to read, and often automate or hide difficult aspects of programming.

Languages for the Web

The languages mentioned so far are most commonly used to develop software for the desktop or for mobile devices. Web technology is a hugely important aspect of computer science and is later explained in much greater depth, it will be useful to introduce you briefly to programming languages for the web.

Web-based applications such as social media sites, news sites, entertainment platforms and other online tools can typically be divided into three parts — databases, server-side software and client-side software. Each of these three parts are most commonly operated using separate languages, although it is possible to use a single language for every aspect. Databases are often accessed using SQL, which is a high-level database querying language. Server-side software, which manages these databases and the data that is sent to the client (user), are usually written in PHP, Ruby or Python (all interpreted languages). Client-side languages are those that make up the pages that are sent to and executed on the user's computer when a web page is received. The most common language here is JavaScript, which provides basic interactivity and animation on the page. This is in addition to CSS (for page formatting) and HTML, which is a mark-up language which specifies how the elements of a web page should appear, and how they should fit together.

As we have just seen, there are numerous programming languages out there; each of them suited to particular tasks. In order to write a program we'll need to know which programming language to use to suit the goal. Now we've got a broad understanding of what a programming language is, and what languages are out there, let us look at the tools we will need to get coding.

What Do I Need?

In order to tell the computer what to do, we need a few things. First, we need a text editor in order to write our code. A common text editor like Notepad or Microsoft Word would be sufficient, but they're not particularly built for writing code in. Microsoft Windows users should use something like 'Programmers Notepad'[1] or 'Notepad++'[2], which are simple to find, install and use. Mac users can find TextWrangler[3] for free on the App Store, but plenty of others are out there. The only purpose of a text editor for programming is to enable us to create, edit and save text files which will store our code.

Second, in order to turn your code into an executable file, we'll need a compiler or an interpreter, which you've just learned about. Depending on the language being used, this will either allow you to run your code as it is (interpret), or translate it (compile) into machine code that can be run without an interpreter. One example is Python — if you need help installing your Python interpreter or finding an appropriate text editor, have a read through Appendix A — Python Development Environment.

Third, you need a basic understanding of the relevant programming language, which is the purpose of this book.

How to Write a Program

As has already been mentioned, the ability to use a programming language is merely the tool used by a programmer to solve problems. A good programmer is not differentiated from a poor programmer by the number of languages they know, in the same way that it is not merely the ability of a carpenter to use a wide range of tools that makes him talented at what he does. We'll now look at a generalised process of developing a program that will help you understand how to use the tools for creating high-quality software.

---

[1] http://www.pnotepad.org/

[2] http://notepad-plus-plus.org/

[3] http://www.barebones.com/products/textwrangler/download.html

The Process

In the development of a computer program, the programmer undertakes a sequence of steps, which develop the program from start to finish. It is helpful to think of a development process as being comprised of a sequence of activities. These activities are:

- Planning,
- Implementation, testing and documentation,
- Deployment and maintenance.

In situations where there are several programmers working on the same project, a range of development models are available to be used, yet for single-developer projects, each of these activities are essential and there are some general remarks to make on each.

Planning is the most essential part of the development process to ensure that the program will be manageable, scalable, efficient and as quick to update as possible. Spend more time planning and you'll save more time later on.

Planning should be done from a general level to a more detailed one. This means, first and foremost, identifying the requirements of the project. Whether it is an employer, customer or you who the project is for, they will typically have some idea of how they want the end product to look, but not fully understand how it needs to be designed. You'll need to learn how to identify incomplete or ambiguous requirements and ask for clarification.

Once the requirements are defined, it's the developer's task to plan the technical design of the program. You need to consider which programming language to use, the structure of your code, and where you can save time by using any available work of third parties. You also need to continually re-evaluate your design to ensure it has the capacity to fully meet the requirements of the project.

Implementation, testing and *documentation* is the meat of the development process. Here you'll actually program the code for your project, while continually verifying that its behaviour is correct. Errors are easier to find and fix as soon as they've been written, not days later; so testing is important at each stage of implementation.

Most development projects can result in relatively large collections of source code (codebases), and remembering how parts of it work or why you made certain design decisions can be challenging. This is where documentation comes in. Use a separate simple text document and comments in your code (explained in the next chapter) to clarify design decisions and to explain what you have coded. This will make it easier to manage large amounts of source code and design efficiently.

Deployment and *maintenance* start as soon as the project has been completed and adequately tested. This will include installation, customisation, verification and a period of evaluation by the user. Straight after deployment, developers need to be prepared for criticism and must have the ability to fix bugs (errors) quickly. Maintaining and enhancing large programs can be time consuming as new faults are found or new features are added.

These activities are likely to appear daunting to beginners. My expectation is not that you will completely understand the development process at this stage, but that having this birds-eye overview of the process will help you understand where the programming principles and knowledge that you learn later fit in to the complete picture.

Now you know a bit about why programming is important to learn, what programming is and the process that computer programmers use to release a piece of software, you're ready to learn the building blocks of a program.

Questions

1. How is a programming language best defined?
2. What is meant by the idea of abstraction?
3. What is machine language?
4. What is the difference between a compiled and an interpreted language?
5. What are the three basic tools you need in order to tell a computer what to do?
6. What are the three main activities you need to carry out in order to develop a piece of software?

Building Blocks

Chapter 2

Variables and Basic Operations

The basic principles and concepts in computer programming are the building blocks for creating powerful and innovative applications. Python is a very straightforward language and has a simple syntax. It will be the language we will use to illustrate the concepts that we pick up along the way. It is designed to allow programmers to create powerful, beautiful code, quickly and enjoyably. You will be able to run the brief examples for yourself using your text editor and Python interpreter, to check they work. The best way to use this book is to read a chapter, then run each of the example programs in that chapter on your own computer. Try changing the code a bit to get a feel for how you can tell the computer what to do. If you had prefer not to worry yet about getting your own Python interpreter installed, repl.it[1] has a really neat online Python text editor and interpreter ready for you to use straight away.

If you are using your own Python interpreter you have two options:

- Input the .py file into your Python interpreter
- Turn your .py file into an executable file

---

[1] http://repl.it/UL8/languages/Python

The first option is executed, using your command line (or terminal on a Mac), as follows:

```
$ python my_file.py
```

The second applies only to Mac and Linux users and requires you to append your .py file with the path to your Python interpreter. Just add the following line to the top of your Python source code to tell your computer that you've written Python code, so you want to execute it using your Python interpreter.

```
#!/usr/bin/python
```

Place this at the top of each Python code file you run. This means you can execute the code without needing to load it into your interpreter when you run it.

If you're using repl.it, you don't need to worry about this. You can execute a program appended as such using the command below where 'my_file.py' is replaced with your code's file name.

```
$ ./my_file.py
```

The ./ here means that the file is found in your current directory (the folder that you are currently using). Alternatively you can simply double-click on the program from within your file explorer.

If you're using Python on a Windows machine, you will just need to double click on the source code file to run it using your Python interpreter.

A 'Hello World' from Python

One of the most basic programs that be written is the age-old 'Hello World' program, so it seems only fitting that this chapter should begin with Python's 'Hello World'. To print a line of text to the screen, just write:

```
print 'Hello World'
```

The output of this program should look like this:

```
$ Hello World
```

Here, the $ symbol is used to denote the output of the program. If you're using repl.it, this will appear as '=>' followed by the output.

Variables

Every mobile application, website, desktop software or embedded system can be thought of as being a program that works with data, whether it is a simple version printing 'Hello World' to a screen, or a very complex version collecting data from satellite imaging and processing it to predict the weather. Even a game, which may not collect data in any way from the real world, operates by performing millions of calculations per second on data inside the program.

Data that is accepted by a program as an input is stored in memory, at a unique *address* so that it can be easily read or changed. If programmers had to remember the locations of all of these variables in memory, the process of programming would be immensely tedious and difficult. Happily, in the main programming language that we'll be looking at, and in most others, the programmer does not need to worry about the address where data is stored. Instead, programming languages allow us to refer to data by a name. Items of data, which are stored in memory and referred to by name, are called *variables.*

Variables are used in programs to store inputted data and calculations that use other variables. The variables can store different types of data. In general, variables are *declared* (created) in three steps:

1. Assign each variable a unique and descriptive name
2. Specify the type of data the variable can hold
3. Assign a value to each variable (numbers or letters)

In Python, we do not always need to declare variables before using them, or declare their type. For example, we can declare a variable as follows:

```
myInteger = 3
```

Python supports two primary types of numbers — *integers* and *floating point numbers.* The above example is a definition of an integer and we have chosen its name to be descriptive of what it is. To define a floating point number, we can use either of the following notations:

```
myFloat = 3.0 # implicit notation
myFloat = float(3) # explicit notation
```

(The # symbol is used in Python for comments. This means that the interpreter ignores anything after that symbol on a line in a Python program. This allows us to write helpful comments next to our code to explain what's going on.)

In programming, words or sentences stored in a variable are called *strings.* They can store any text that you may need in your program. Strings are defined in Python using either single or double quotation marks:

```
myString = ‘this is a string’
myString = “this is a string”
```

In order to include actual quotation marks inside your string without them terminating the string, you can use a backslash (\) before the quotation mark. Alternatively, if your string is encapsulated with single quotes, you can use double quotes inside your string without needing to use a backslash:

```
myString = ‘“Yes”, isn\’t he strange.’
$ “Yes”, isn’t he strange.
```

In addition to strings and integers and floating point numbers, a common and hugely useful type of variable in Python is the *list.* A list is a collection of other variables of any data type and of any length. A list is similar to an array in other languages, but is more flexible. A list is first declared, and then populated as follows:

```
myList = [] # declaration of list
myList.append(12)
myList.append("text")
myList.append(10000)
print "The first element of the list is: " + str(myList[0])
$ The first element of the list is: 12
print myList # prints the whole contents of the list
$ [12, text, 1000]
```

Lists can also be declared and populated in one step, in-line:

```
myList = [1, 2, 3] # declaration of list and content
print myList # prints the whole contents of the list
$ [1, 2, 3]
```

The final important variable that we're going to look at is the Python *dictionary* object. A dictionary is an object which matches a key with a value. It is a kind of list but elements are accessed not by its index, but by a key.

```
phonebook = {
    "James" : 09386477566,
    "Harry" : 09383377264,
    "Sophie" : 09472662781 }
print phonebook["James"]
$ 09386477566
```

Take the example of a phonebook as in the example above. Here we have a name, matched up with a phone number. When we print the element in the dictionary 'phonebook' with the key 'James', the dictionary locates the value corresponding to that key and prints James's phone number.

Dictionaries are useful for storing a wide range of data in many different situations, such as matching words to definitions, matching names to phone numbers or matching car registration numbers to makes and models.

Basic Operations

Common number-crunching programs are spreadsheets, database software and games. String manipulation is performed on social media websites, word processors and language translators. When programming, these kind of manipulations are generally referred to as *operations*. These are simple processes that data undergoes in order to form part of some kind of computation.

Some simple operations are performed on strings and numbers in these programs, and are built up to form complex equations or sets of powerful instructions.

Basic mathematical operations can be performed on numbers:

```
firstInt = 1
secondInt = 2
addInt = firstInt + secondInt
subtractInt = firstInt – secondInt
multiplyInt = firstInt * secondInt
divideFloat = float(firstInt) / float(secondInt)
print addInt, subtractInt, multiplyInt, divideFloat #
  prints all
$ 3 -1 2 0.5
```

Above, we have surrounded the variables 'firstInt' and 'secondInt' with brackets and used the word 'float' before them. This *casts* the integers as floating point numbers in order that we can perform division on them.

A *power operation* is one which multiplies a number by itself a certain number of times. For example 2^3 is 8 ($2 \times 2 \times 2$). In order to perform a power operation, we can use two multiplication symbols:

```
powerInt = 3 ** 2 # 3 to the power of 2
print powerInt
$ 9
```

Another operator which may be unfamiliar to you is the modulo (%) operator, which returns the integer remainder of a division.

```
remainder = 11 % 3 # integer remainder after 11 is divided by 3
print remainder
$ 2
```

In addition to numerical operators being used to perform calculations, Python provides excellent features for string manipulation which form new strings, as illustrated by the following example:

```
greeting = "Hello"
name = "Tom"
personalGreeting = greeting + "," + name
print personalGreeting
$ Hello, Tom
```

Here we have added two explicitly declared strings together — `greeting` and `name` — with an implicit string in the middle (", "). The process of adding strings in this way to form new string is called *concatenation.*

Trying to concatenate numbers within strings in Python will not work:

```
number = 5
string = 'hello'
combined = number + string
$ Traceback (most recent call last):
    File "<stdin>", line 3, in <module>
  TypeError: unsupported operand type(s) for +: 'int' and 'str'
```

The output of this program is a Python error which tells us that the operator '+' does not support operands of type 'int' and 'str' (string) together. However, we can *cast* an integer to a string without needing to declare a new variable:

```
number = 5
string = 'hello'
combined = str(number) + string
$ 5 hello
```

The *function* (functions will be explained later) str() can be used to convert an integer or floating point number to a string on the fly, so that we can print numbers alongside strings using concatenation.

The multiplication operator (*) can be used with a string and a number as well as two numbers and behaves by repeating the string by the value of the number:

```
repeatedText = ‘Hello‘ * 5
print repeatedText
$ Hello Hello Hello Hello Hello
```

We can also use the *increment* ‘+=’ and *decrement* ‘–=’ operators to add a specified value to a number variable. These operators add or subtract their operand to a number respectively. For example:

```
number1 = 0
number1 += 1
print ‘number1 is‘ + str(number1)
number1 -= 7
print ‘number1 is‘ + str(number1)
$ number1 is 1
$ number1 is -6
```

These are particularly useful for performing basic mathematical calculations on data in a program and you’ll use them often.

Input and Output

Software is useless unless it does something with the data it has processed. This often means that data is collected in some way, processed and then displayed to the user. For the time being, our use of Pythons Input and Output (I/O) features will be primarily for learning to use the language and process data, but at a later stage we will use text or numerical input and text- or graphics-based outputs.

As we've already seen to output a string to the command line in Python, we use:

```
print 'this is some text'
```

However this only gives us a limited capability. What about if we want to print lots of different variables in the same line? Python allows us to add placeholders for variables inside the main string to be printed and then specify the variables at the end. For example:

```
print 'My name is %s and I weigh %d kg' % ('Joe Bloggs', 80)
$ My name is Joe Bloggs and I weigh 80 kg
```

In this example, %s depicts the placeholder for a string and %d specifies the location for a number. The variables are then listed in the order in which they should appear, inside the brackets, separated from the string by a % symbol. This technique can be extended to include any number of variables inside a string to be printed.

All software accepts some kind of input, whether it is from a sensor, the Internet or a human. When learning to write programs and when designing them professionally, it's important, therefore, to understand how to get basic input from a user.

Python here offers us the `input()` function allowing us to ask the user for some kind of information and to collect their reply.

```
person = input("Please enter your name: ")
print "Your name is: " + person
$ Please enter your name:
  Joe # Entered by the user
$ Your name is: Joe
```

By default, the string entered by the user will always be a string. If you require the user to enter a number, such as their age, you'll need to convert their entry into a number as follows:

```
ageString = input("Please enter your age: ")
ageNumber = int(ageString)
```

```
print "You are" + ageNumber + "years old."
$ Please enter your age:
  42 # Entered by the user
$ You are 42 years old.
```

We now have the basic skills required to accept, process and output basic user data, but we've only looked at performing basic calculations and string manipulation so far. In order to make our programs more interesting and powerful, we need to introduce the ability to perform repeated tasks and make intelligent decisions based upon the data we have.

Questions

1. How does the data type integer differ from a floating point number?
2. Should the value of a string be declared in single quotes or double quotes when it is set?
3. How does the list data type differ from the dictionary data type in Python?
4. What symbol must you use in order to perform a 'to the power of' operation in Python? Write down a program which prints the value of 3 to the power of 7.
5. What do the increment and decrement operators do?
6. When outputting a string to the screen, what's the difference between the placeholders %d and %s?

Chapter 3

Decisions and Loops

One of the variables that we left out in Chapter 2, was the *Boolean* variable, or *bool* for short. This is a variable that can have only two possible values — true or false.

We've seen that a number variable can be assigned a value based upon the value of previously declared variables, for example, `z = x + y`. This example *evaluates* the sum of `x` and `y` and assigns it to `z`. The same can be done with Booleans — we can evaluate an expression that can either be true or false, and assign the result to a Boolean variable.

Conditions

A condition is something that can be evaluated as true or false, depending on the values of the variables, and the symbols used in the condition's expression. The following demonstrates the equality condition (==), which is true if the operands are equal in value.

```
x = 1
y = 'hello'
print x == 1
print y == 'hello'
$ True
$ True
```

The operand '!=' is equivalent to 'not equal' and is true if the operands are not equal to each other.

```
x = 1
y = 'hello'
print x != 2
print y == 'goodbye'
$ False
$ False
```

Variables can be compared to each other in size using the inequality operators < ('less than'), > ('greater than'), <= ('less than or equal to') or >= ('greater than or equal to').

```
x = 1
y = 2
print x < 2
print y >= 3
$ True
$ False
```

If the Boolean expression requires several conditions to be met it can include the keywords '`and`' and '`or`'. For example:

```
x = 1
y = 2
print x < 2 and y > 4 # First condition met, second not
  met so false
print y >= 3 or x ==1 # First condition not met, second
  met, so true
$ False
$ True
```

The '`and`' keyword requires both expressions to be met, but the '`or`' keyword requires either expression to be met in order for the whole condition to be true.

To invert a Boolean output, the '`not`' keyword can be used. For example:

```
x = 1
print not False
print not x == 1
$ True
$ False
```

The final keyword that we need to look at is the '`in`' keyword. This operator is used to check if a given value is found in a Python list. We saw in Chapter 2 how to create and append lists to contain lots of items of data. The '`in`' keyword looks at a list of elements, and is 'true' if the list contains a value equal to the operand. The following example illustrates how this works:

```
myList = ["Jack", "Jill"]
print "Jack" in myList
print "Harry" in myList
$ True
$ False
```

The 'if' Statement

The next aspect of programming that we will look at is decision making. In human language we make decisions by comparing the different options available to us, and choosing which we prefer. For instance, if the sun is clear and the air is warm, then just wear a T-shirt. Or else, if the sky is clear but the air is cold, then wear a jumper. Or else, if the sky is not clear, but the air is warm wear a coat. Or else, if the sky is not clear and the air is cold, wear a coat and a jumper.

Although for humans this is often a subconscious routine, computers use a similar process of working through sets of predefined logical processes in order to make decisions and get things done.

In human language we use the word 'if' when explaining our decision making. Python uses the same keyword *if.* If a Boolean expression — a condition that evaluates as a Boolean — is true, Python executes a certain block of code. If it is not true (in Boolean *else*), another block of code may be executed.

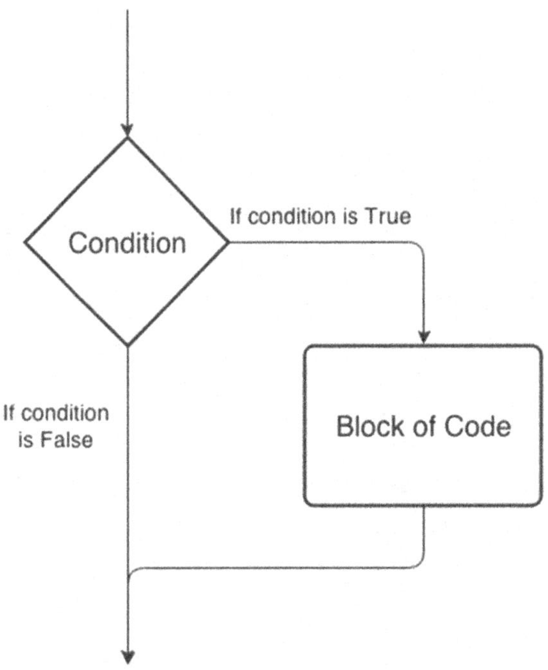

The diagram above makes this clear. It demonstrates the flow of logic for a simple 'if' statement with no 'else' clause. Let us have a look at the basic syntax in Python:

```
if <expression evaluates to true>:
       <execute this code>
       ...
       ...
elif <this expression evaluates to true>:
       <execute this code>
       ...
       ...
```

```
else:
        <execute this code>
        ...
        ...
```

Put into words, this is read as 'if the first condition is true, execute the first block of code, else if ('elif') the second condition is true, execute the second block of code, else (in all other circumstances) execute the third block of code'. If the first condition is met, the first block of code is executed, and the last two are ignored. If the first condition is not met but the second condition is, the second block of code is executed and the third ignored. Only if neither condition is met, will the third block of code be executed.

At this stage it will be helpful to explain *indentation* and *blocks* in Python. A block of code is a sequence of instructions that are executed at a certain point in a program. This may be some set of instructions inside an 'if' statement, or inside a loop, as we'll see shortly. Python separates blocks of code from each other using indentation.

```
x = 1
y = 2
if x == 1:
        # This is a block of code
        print 'x equals 1'
        print 'y equals ' + str(y)
$ x equals 1
$ y equals 2
```

As you can see in the example above, two 'print' commands are indented to ensure they are understood by the interpreter as a block of code to be executed if and only if the condition is met. Lines of code can be indented in Python using the TAB key on your keyboard, or by entering 4 spaces. Indentation is very important in Python. If your code is not correctly indented, it will not be correctly interpreted. Do not worry too much at this stage about when to indent your code, as you will soon get a feel for it when you read some more examples in later chapters.

The 'if' statement can be used separately from 'elif' or 'else' in cases where a single condition needs to be tested and there is only one block of code for that single condition. Thus the user can use 'if' as in the indentation example above.

However, if the problem you are trying to solve requires one of two actions depending on a pair of conditions, you can use 'if' and 'elif' without using 'else', as in this example:

```
names = ["George", "Hannah", "Mike"]
if "Fred" in names:
       print 'Fred is on the list'
elif "Hannah" in names:
       print 'Hannah is in names'
$ Hannah is in names
```

Alternatively, 'if' and 'else' can be used when a single condition requires testing and some action is required if it's not met:

```
names = ["George", "Hannah", "Mike"]
if "Fred" in names:
       print 'Fred is on the list'
else:
       print 'Fred is not on the list'
$ Fred is not on the list
```

As you will have noticed, when a prior expression is met, the remaining expressions in the 'if...else' block are not tested, since the block corresponding to the first satisfied condition is executed. If multiple blocks need to be executed for different conditions, multiple 'if...else' statements can be used.

```
names = ["George", "Hannah", "Mike"]
if "Fred" in names:
       print 'Fred is on the list'
```

```
else:
      print 'Fred is not on the list'
if "George" in names:
      print 'George is on the list'
else:
      print 'George is not on the list'
if "Hannah" in names:
      print 'Hannah is on the list'
else:
      print 'Hannah is not on the list'

$ Fred is not on the list
$ George is on the list
$ Hannah is on the list
```

The 'for' Loop

In addition to the above 'evaluating conditions', one of the most commonly used concepts in programming is the loop. This is a command for when tasks need to be repeated several times. For example, you may have a list of names (as above) and need to print out a list of all the names in the list. Instead of manually typing out commands to separately print each element of the list, you can use a loop to iterate over the list, and perform the `print` command on each element. Thus, we can replace the following:

```
names = ["George", "Hannah", "Mike"]
print names[0]
print names[1]
print names[2]

$ George
$ Hannah
$ Mike
```

with an operationally identical block, using a '*for*' loop.

```
names = ["George", "Hannah", "Mike"]
for name in names:
       print name

$ George
$ Hannah
$ Mike
```

In this example, we have only saved one line of text, but for larger lists we can perform operations much faster using loops.

The flow of logic is illustrated in the diagram below.

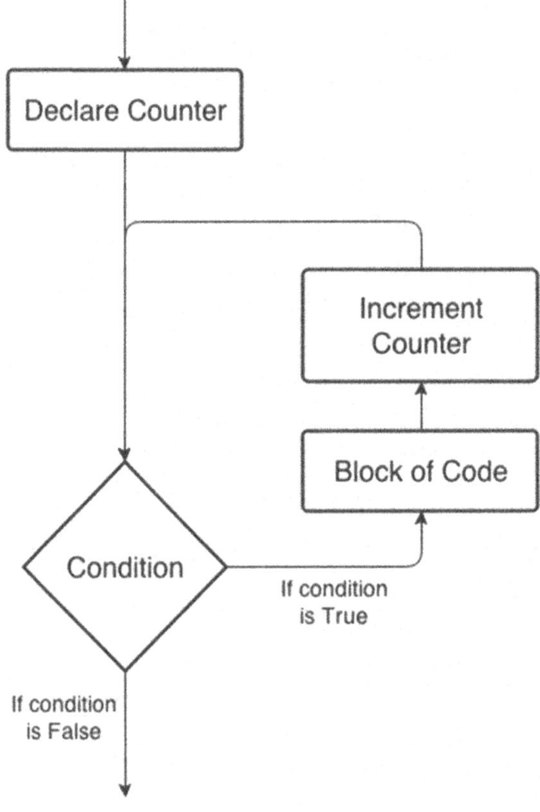

So, a counter is defined and the loop's condition is tested. If the condition is satisfied, the contained block of code is executed and the counter is incremented. Unlike most programing languages, Python hides the incrementing for us. The keyword 'in' causes Python to automatically iterate over the range specified by incrementing a counter.

The above example uses the '`for <iterator> in <list>:`' syntax which is helpful when we don't know the length of a list. However, we can also use the operator 'for' to loop over a block a specific number of times. For instance, to print consecutive numbers to the screen, we can do the following:

```
for x in range(0, 5):
  print 'This is line %d' % (x)


$ This is line 0
$ This is line 1
$ This is line 2
$ This is line 3
$ This is line 4
```

In Python — and in most other programming languages — lists (including a 'range' in a 'for' loop) begin with the "0th" element. So the above example performs a loop of increasing 'x' from `x = 0` to `x = 4`, therefore running five times as specified.

We can also 'nest' loops inside other loops in order to execute a certain function on each iteration (in this case, an iteration is one cycle of the loop) of the outer loop.

```
for x in range(0, 3):
      for y in range (0, 2):
            print 'This is line %d, column %d' % (x, y)


$ This is line 0 column 0
$ This is line 0 column 1
$ This is line 1 column 0
```

```
$ This is line 1 column 1
$ This is line 2 column 0
$ This is line 2 column 1
```

Here, the outer loop takes the number variable x from `x = 0` to `x = 2`, and for each value of `x`, the number variable y has first the value `y = 0`, then the value `y = 1`, since the inner loop takes the variable from `y = 0` to `y = 1`.

The 'while' Loop

The 'while' loop is similar to the 'for' loop, except that the duration of its looping is not always predefined before the loop begins. The 'while' loop continues to loop for as long as its condition is evaluated as true, as shown in the illustration below:

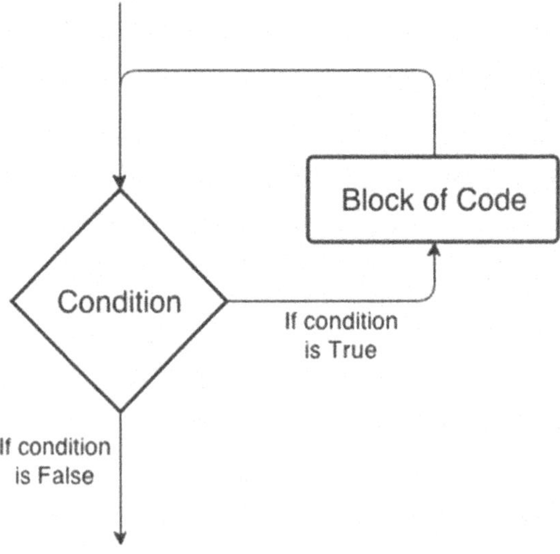

The basic syntax for the Python 'while' loop is:

```
while <expression is true>:
      <execute this code>
```

The expression here can be anything we have seen previously which evaluates to a Boolean. If the expression is false, the loop is ended and the program's execution resumes with the next instruction after the block inside the 'while' loop. The following example illustrates this behaviour:

```
print 'This is a line of code that is executed'
name = 'James'
while nameEntered != name:
      print name + " has not been entered yet"
      nameEntered = input("Enter your name here: ")
print name + " has been entered so the 'while' loop
  stopped"
```

```
$ James has not been entered
$ Enter your name here:
 Jack
$ James has not been entered
$ Enter your name here:
 James
$ James has been entered so the 'while' loop stopped
```

Here the loop is resumed until the user enters 'James' as their name, since, when they do, the condition of the 'while' loop is no longer satisfied, so the loop is broken.

The Keywords 'break' and 'continue'

When using 'for' and/or 'while' loops in Python, you may want to exit a particular loop if a certain event occurs, or a certain condition is met that is different from the loop's condition. Alternatively, you may need the rest of the current block in a loop to be skipped and the next loop to begin.

The Python 'break' keyword quits the loop in which it is found. The 'continue' keyword stops executing the rest of the block inside a loop in which the keyword is found, and resumes from the beginning of the loop at the next cycle. Thus:

```
count = 0
while True:
        print count
        count += 1
        if count >= 5:
        break;
$ 0
$ 1
$ 2
$ 3
$ 4
$ 5
```

In the example above, the variable `count` is incremented by 1, using the operator '+='. With each cycle of the loop the variable `count` is tested to see if it is bigger than 5. If it is, the loop breaks, and the program exits.

```
count = 0
for x in range(10):
        # Check if x is even
        if x % 2 == 0:
                continue
        print x
$ 1
$ 3
$ 5
```

In this 'for' loop, the remainder operator % calculates the remainder after dividing `x` with 2. If the remainder is 1, `x` is odd, the expression resolves to false and the loop proceeds to complete by printing `x`. If the remainder is 0, `x` is even and the loop continues, skipping the ‘`print x`’ instruction.

Questions

1. Which Boolean value would the following expression evaluate to: `((4 =< 2) and (True != False))`?
2. What does the ‘in’ operator do?
3. Write a small program which asks the user for their age, and if their age is 17 or greater, prints the string “You are old enough to drive”, otherwise it prints “You are too young to drive”.
4. In the context of a ‘while’ loop, what do the ‘break’ and ‘continue’ keywords do?

Chapter 4
Functions

So far, we have looked at the basic components of a computer program, including variables, operations, conditionals and loops. These are the foundation of any program you will write. However, each program we've written so far has only a single linear set of instructions, after which the program finished. It is time to introduce functions.

Functions are fundamental to computer programs. They are a way of dividing code into blocks that can be reused when needed. Functions allow code to be more manageable, more readable and more powerful in its capabilities.

In Chapter 1, we explored the notion of abstraction and saw that it allows engineers and computer scientists to hide trivial low-level computations away in order to provide, more simply, powerful capabilities to higher-level aspects of a system. In software development 'functions' are the primary means of abstraction.

In a function, a predefined set of instructions are specified which are to be performed each time the function is 'called'. The 'calling' of a function can be thought of as one part of your code, requesting that the code inside that function be executed. Typically a function will have an input, an operation and an output, and in this sense it is equivalent to a mini- or sub-program. The *inputs* to a function are typically referred to as *parameters* or *arguments.* These parameters can be any kind of data represented as Python variables such as Booleans, numbers, strings, lists, dictionaries, objects (which we will cover later) and others. They are passed into the function when it is called. The *operation* of a function is specified as a set of instructions which may perform operations on the inputs, or otherwise may manipulate data held outside of the function and not given as parameters. The *output* of a function is known as the function's *return value*. This is a value which is specified as a result of the operation of the function and is assigned to a variable when the function is called.

The following example illustrates the basic syntax for defining and executing a Python function:

```
# Function is defined
def <function_name>(<parameters separated with commas>):
       <do something>
       …
       return <output>

# Function is called
output = <function_name> (parameter1, …, parameterN)
print output # Return value of the function is printed to
  the screen

$ <return value of function_name>
```

This may look a bit daunting at first, but Python functions are a very simple and intuitive construct. The keyword 'def' stands for definition and denotes a function. The next word is the user-defined name for the function. The brackets immediately following the function name contain a list of parameter names. The operation of the function is then specified, and a variable is returned.

The function is called outside the definition of the function and is given some parameters as inputs. The function's return value is assigned to the variable 'output' and is then printed to the screen. It is important to note that a function is not executed at the point in the code at which it is defined. A function is only executed when it is called.

Functions are not required to accept parameters or output a return value, or even perform any meaningful computation as their operation. Let us look, for instance, at the following example of a basic function in Python:

```
def my_function:
       print 'my_function says "Hello"!'
my_function()

$ my_function says "Hello"!
```

This example accepts no parameters and so does not have a pair of brackets after its name. Rather, the only operation of this function is to print a string to the screen. The function is defined in line one, and the indented block of code shows that it simply executes one 'print' command. Neither does it have a return value, so it does not use the Python keyword 'return'. The function is called in line three at which point it is executed and the output displays the string printed to the screen.

The greeting from `my_function` in the example above was a little impersonal. The next example demonstrates the use of parameters as inputs to the function.

```
def my_function(name):
       print 'my_function says "Hello %s"!' % (name)

myName = input('Enter your name: ')
my_personal_function(myName)

$ Enter your name:
  Fred
$ my_function says "Hello Fred"!
```

The use of the parameter inside the function should be clear. The function definition calls the input parameter 'name' and inserts it into a more personal greeting from out function. Outside the function definition, the user is asked for their name and the string they enter is stored in the variable 'myName'. Our new function 'my_personal_functon' is called, and the user's name is pasted in. The function then executes, and prints the personal greeting to the screen.

Now we've mastered the concept of an input parameter let's go for a mathematical example, and write a basic summing function with a return value.

```
def sum_two_numbers(a, b):
        sum = a + b
        print 'The sum of %d and %d is %d' % (a, b, sum)
        return sum

# Parameters given here
returnValue = sum_two_numbers(4, 7) # sum assigned to
  returnValue
print 'The function has returned %d' % (returnValue)

$ The sum of 4 and 7 is 11
$ The function has returned 11
```

Note that there are three previously unseen features to this example. First, our function accepts two parameters instead of just one. In Python any number of parameters can be passed into a function when it is called, as long as the number of parameters passed into the function matches the amount the function is expecting. Second, our input parameters are specified in the same line as the function is called, instead of being specified previously by being assigned to a variable. Third, this example returns a value — the numerical sum of the two parameters. When the function returns after being called, the next line of code prints the variable 'returnValue' to the screen, which has a value equal to 'sum' inside the function, since it is assigned the return value.

You may have noticed that in our last function 'sum_two_numbers', we did perform some degree of abstraction. We took two operations — addition and printing — and abstracted them away into a function which can be called repeatedly with a single line:

```
sum1 = sum_two_numbers(4, 7) # sum assigned to returnValue
sum2 = sum_two_numbers(2, 12) # sum assigned to returnValue
sum3 = sum_two_numbers(34, 121) # sum assigned to returnValue
```

```
$ The sum of 4 and 7 is 11
$ The sum of 2 and 12 is 14
$ The sum of 34 and 121 is 155
```

Having previously defined this function, we are able to run the three lines of code in the box above, to perform the addition and printing of three different pairs of numbers. You can see that for more complex numerical operations, this concept of abstraction using functions can be extremely powerful.

A Bigger and Better Example

Now is a good time for our knowledge of functions to be combined with what we know already about variables and conditions. We're going to design a function which performs a range of calculations on two input variables; that is, we are going to design a calculator.

For a programmer, the ability to think in a *top-down* sense is vitally important. This means that you must be able to understand what your primary goal is and what lower-level operations need to be abstracted away as functions in order to meet your requirements.

So, our goal is to build a function which accepts three parameters — two numbers and a string — and performs the correct calculation on these numbers depending on the value of the string. Thinking in our top-down way, we can see that our primary requirement is a function with the following form:

```
def calculator(a, b, operation):
       <perform calculation>
       return result
```

To be a calculator, our program must perform addition, subtraction, multiplication, division and power operations. The operation of the calculator depends on the value of the parameter 'operation'.

From this information about our goal, we're able to deduce that inside the 'calculator' function, we need to make some kind of decision based upon the value of the string 'operation'.

Therefore, without specifying the exact operations of the functions 'add', 'subtract', 'multiply', 'divide' or 'power', we know that our 'calculator' function must take a form similar to the one below.

```
def calculator(a, b, operation):
        if operation == 'add':
                result = add(a, b)
        elif operation == 'subtract':
                result = subtract(a, b)
        elif operation == 'multiply':
                result = multiply(a, b)
        elif operation == 'divide':
                result = divide(a, b)
        elif operation == 'power':
                result = power(a, b)
        else:
                result = 0
        return result
```

Here the value of the parameter 'operation' is tested. A variable 'result' is assigned the return value of one of the — as yet undefined — functions, determined by the operation to be performed. We can simply define these functions as the following:

```
def add(a, b):
        return a + b

def subtract(a, b):
        return a - b

def multiply(a, b):
        return a*b
```

```
def divide(a, b):
        return a/b

def power(a, b):
        result = a
        for x in range(b):
                result = result*a
        return result
```

All of these functions take the two number variables 'a' and 'b' as their input parameters and return a value. The first four should be self-explanatory to you, however the last may not be. The function 'power' is required to return the value of 'a' to the power of 'b'. In other words it should return 'a' multiplied by itself 'b' times. This is implemented using a loop which — after setting 'result' equal to 'a' — multiplies 'a' by 'result' 'b' times. Then, when the loop finishes, the value of 'result' is returned.

We can now combine all these function definitions together into a single file, in order to complete our calculator.

```
def add(a, b):
        return a + b
def subtract(a, b):
        return a – b
def multiply(a, b):
        return a*b
def divide(a, b):
        return a/b
def power(a, b):
        result = a
        for x in range(b):
                result = result*a
        return result
def calculator(a, b, operation):
        if operation == 'add':
```

```
            result = add(a, b)
        elif operation == 'subtract':
            result = subtract(a, b)
        elif operation == 'multiply':
            result = multiply(a, b)
        elif operation == 'divide':
            result = divide(a, b)
        elif operation == 'power':
            result = power(a, b)
        else:
            result = 0
        return result

print '5 plus 2 is ' + str(calculator(5, 2, 'add'))
print '1 minus 7 is ' + str(calculator(1, 7, 'subtract'))
print '3 times 8 is ' + str(calculator(3, 8, 'multiply'))
print '2 divided by 2 is ' + str(calculator(2, 2, 'divide'))
print '3 to the power of 2 is ' + str(calculator(3, 2,
  'power'))
```

```
$ 5 plus 2 is 7
$ 1 minus 7 is -6
$ 3 times 8 is 24
$ 2 divided by 2 is 1
$ 3 to the power of 2 is 9
```

Here we've simply placed all our previously defined functions into a single file, and called the 'calculator' function five times, to demonstrate each mode of operation. With each 'print' command, we're printing the explanation of the calculation, concatenated with the return value of the calculator, converted to a string using 'str'.

You will now recognise 'str( )' as a function. Each time we have called 'str( )' or, previously, 'int( )', we are using functions that are predefined for us. They are functions which accept a parameter and return, respectively, the 'string value' or 'integer value' representation of the input parameter, by performing an operation on it. As we progress through future chapters of this book we will use many different functions, some of which we'll write, others of which are built in to the Python interpreter, and still others we will import from 'libraries'.

One of the powerful things that a function provides is reusability. We can call a function as many times as we need to. If we can call a function that we've written, can we not also allow others to reuse our code to save their time? And use the codes of others to save ours? Well: yes we can! This continuation of the idea of abstraction is explored in different ways much more fully in later chapters but, it is worth understanding here that the power available to you through coding does not require you to do everything yourself. You are able immediately to use the high-level functions that others have written, which can provide you with extremely powerful capabilities. These are collections of functions and objects that give your software capabilities created beforehand by someone else.

Questions

1. How would you describe what a function is, in the simplest way?
2. What are a function's parameters used for?
3. What is a function's return value used for?
4. How can functions be used to break down a complex problem into smaller manageable blocks?
5. Write a function which accepts three parameters as numbers, and returns the value of the sum of the three numbers. Call this function in your Python script and print the output to the screen.

Taking it Further

Chapter 5

Classes and Objects

You know what a model car or a model plane is. They are the small replicas we put together and painted as children. But the fact is that *models are ubiquitous.* Banks use financial models to predict stock price movement. Weather forecasting is done by extrapolating the output of ocean and atmospheric models. The enterprise of science is an attempt to develop sophisticated models to describe and predict the physical behaviour of the natural universe. Engineers use models to create and test designs for engines, computer chips and robots.

In all of these cases, when I refer to models I am referring to a computer model or a computer program. It is software that predicts the weather, not a human. It is software that buys and sells thousands of shares every millisecond, not a human. It is software which guides a rocket out of the atmosphere and puts it on the moon, not a human. And that means that it is programmers who design the software-based models of physical realities in order to solve many of the problems facing society today.

Object-Oriented Programming

Python is an *object-oriented* programming (OOP) language which means that it provides features which support OOP. OOP is a programming concept used in the creation of most modern software, designed to simplify the development of complex programs and make code more manageable, reliable and understandable.

We have not called it such, but up until now, we have been writing basic ***procedural programs*** which have their focus on writing procedures operating on some data. In OOP, the focus shifts from procedures to ***objects***. You can think of an object as a model, containing both the data and functionality required to model a real world object, and they are designed to interact with each other in the same way that real world objects do.

In procedural programming we might write a function such as `countNumberOfSubstringOccurrences(some_string, some_test_string)` which suggests that the function is the active agent. We're effectively saying to the Python interpreter, "Hey Python, here's a random string, can you count how many occurrences of this substring there are in it?"

In OOP however, it is objects that are considered the active agent. That is, it is the *object* we are commanding to perform some action. Now, we might do the following:

```
some_string = 'the cat sat on the mat'
some_sub_string = 'a'
print some_string.count(some_sub_string)
$ 3
```

This short program uses the fact that a string in Python is an object, which has a method (function) called 'count'. This method accepts a string and returns a number which, in this case, is the number of times the string occurs in the object string. The methods of objects are accessed using the 'dot notation' exemplified above. The object ('some_string'), used in the example above, is a Python string object. We therefore have access to all the methods that the Python string has, including the 'count' method. We specify the name of the object followed by a dot followed by the method name to execute the method on that object.

It may not be immediately obvious why this change in perspective is useful, but it turns out that this shift from focusing on procedures to focusing on objects allows us greater versatility when writing programs. When we think about it, this concept matches very closely with our experiences in life. When we want to call someone we do not use our microwave, we use a phone. So a phone can be modelled as having a 'call' method. But if we were modelling a microwave, it would not have that method, but a 'cook' method instead. OOP allows us to mirror real world objects in order to model them and solve problems which are related to them.

Objects don't even need to exist in reality. They could be highly abstract ideas that you may need to create, such as a 'Connection' object, or a 'DatabaseHandler' object. These are objects which would have variables — known as attributes — and methods, but don't physically exist. A 'Connection' object could be used to manage a connection to a server over the Internet, and the 'DatabaseHandler' may contain methods for reading and writing data to a database.

In Python, every variable is an object, whether it is an integer, a dictionary or a duck-billed platypus. Programs manipulate objects by performing computations with them, or asking them to perform methods. It is helpful to think of an object having both a *state* and a collection of *methods*, that it can perform. The state of the object, represents everything that we know about an object, such as a platypus's size, colour, age and current direction of travel. A platypus, for example, has the ability to move in different directions, to eat, to sleep and eventually to die. These actions can be modelled as methods and each of these methods will change the state of the object. If it has a 'moveForward' method, its position, direction and age will be changed by the time the method has completed.

Defining Objects using Classes

You may have already guessed that Python does not have a built-in 'platypus' object. We've already used many of the built-in Python variables, such as strings, integers, floats and lists, yet in many cases we need to create objects which relate specifically to the problem we're trying to solve.

A *class* in Python, is a template for an object. It specifies the attributes and methods that every *instance* of that class should have. To think of it in a different way, an object is an instance of a class — something which uses the template of a class but has its own individual state.

When programming using an OOP language, we will typically create 'classes' to model a real world object and then create objects which are instances of those real world objects. For example, I could create a class to describe a human that would have the instance attributes 'position', 'name', 'age' and 'gender' among others, and could have methods such as 'walkUpOneUnit' and 'changeName'. I would then create instances of this class which represented different people. For example I could create an instance of the class 'Human' whose attribute 'name' was set to 'Dave', whose height was 190cm and so forth. From here many such objects could be made that all have the same variables and methods, but a different state, since each attribute would be different for each object.

We can model a 'Position' as an object with two attributes — and x-position and y-position. We can define a 'Position' object by writing a new class:

```
class Position:
  def __init__(self, x, y):
      self.xPosition = x;
      self.yPosition = y;
  def getXPos(self):
      return self.x
  def getYPos(self):
      return self.y
  def setXPos(self, newX):
      self.x = newX
  def setYPos(self, newY):
      self.y = newY
```

You will be wondering at this point what the '__init__' function is all about. In Python, as in most OOP languages, this is an example of a 'constructor'. It is a function that is called automatically when an instance of a class is made. When, in this case, a new 'position' object is made, its attributes need to be initialised to the required values. For example to create a 'Position' object at the position (3, 7), we would create an instance of this class and set `x = 3` and `y = 7`. The 'self' keyword in the list of arguments for the constructor represents the object itself, and is present in the argument list for every method in a class. Here's our new Position object:

```
myPosition = Position(3, 7)
```

In our example of a class (above), we've defined four methods for the 'Position' object — 'getXPos', 'getYPos', 'setXPos' and 'setYPos'. Having created our object 'myPosition', we can get the x- and y-positions of the object by calling the method on the object.

```
print myPosition.getXPos()
print myPosition.getYPos()
$ 3
$ 7
```

We can, then set them to new values as follows:

```
myPosition.setXPos(2)
myPosition.setYPos(9)
print myPosition.getXPos()
print myPosition.getYPos()
$ 2
$ 9
```

To clarify — we first defined a class to model a position and named it 'Position'. We then created a position object called 'myPosition', set its initial values, and printed them to check they were set. We then used two more of the object's methods to set new values for the *x*- and *y*-coordinates of the object, and printed them out.

Using the example from before, a 'Human' can be modelled as having a host of attributes describing their state, and one of these could be, for instance, their position in space. Now that we understand what a class is, we can define a new class which will itself contain a 'Position' object as an attribute.

```
class Human:
       def __init__(self, initPosition, initAge, initName,
initGender):
              self.position = initPosition;
              self.age = initAge;
              self.name = initName;
              self.gender = initGender;

       def printDetails(self):
              print self.name + "'s age is " + str(self.age) +
"and gender is " + self.gender + "."
       detailsString = ""
       if self.gender == 'male':
              detailsString += 'He '
       else:
              detailsString += 'She '
       stringAddition = 'is at position (%d, %d).' %
(self.position.getXPos(), self.position.getYPos())
       detailsString += stringAddition
       print detailsString
```

Now that we have defined these two classes, we can create an *instance* of 'Human', called 'Dave'.

```
davesPosition = Position(7, 2)
davesObject = Human(davesPosition, 43, 'Dave', 'male')
davesObject.printDetails()
print davesObject.name
$ Dave's age is 43 and is male.
$ He is at position (7, 2)
$ Dave
```

In defining the 'Human' class, we specified the attributes that each 'Human' object should have. We also defined a method which prints the contents of that object to the screen. You should be able to work your way through that method and see what is happening. Try comparing the output of this program in the box above with the earlier 'printDetails' method, making sure you understand how we got there. (If you try running this code yourself, make sure that both the 'Position' and 'Human' classes, as well as the code above which creates the objects, are in the same file. Otherwise, if you just try executing the three lines of code above, the Python interpreter won't know where to find our classes and will give an error.)

The final line of the example code above reads `print davesObject.name`. We can access the attributes of an object using the same dot notation as we use for accessing its methods. When attributes are initialised in the constructor of the class, they become available to be accessed from outside the object using this notation.

Inheritance

There are a number of different relationships in the real world between one object and another, both in their behaviour and in their design. Both in terms of design and behaviour, a pen is a very different object to a piece of paper, however they interact when the pen writes on the paper.

To take a separate example from cricket, a batter in a match is different to a bowler in his or her behaviour, but not in his or her design. The way in which the batter interacts with other objects is very different to the way in which the bowler does so, but as human beings they are designed very similarly.

In OOP, this concept is called *inheritance*. This is an object-oriented concept in which design and behaviour (attributes and methods) are inherited from other objects. This allows two classes to inherit from another parent class, thus sharing a common derivative in terms of their most fundamental attributes and methods.

To take a basic example: every animal has a weight and a height. There is no animal that does not have these attributes. A lion is an animal and so inherits all of these attributes from being an animal, but a lion has a mane and a tail in addition to these basic attributes.

If we were to write classes that model 'lions', 'goats' and 'camels', we would need to make a comprehensive list of all of the attributes that are possessed by each of these animals. Many of these features would be repeated, as they are common to many or all of them.

Inheritance allows us to design an 'animal' class and then write a 'lion' class, a 'sheep' class and a 'camel' class, each of which belong to the 'animal' class. This means that they *automatically* have all the attributes given to the 'animal' class. We can then add features and behaviour that are specific to each of the individual animal classes.

Taking the example of a batter and a bowler in a game of Cricket, we're going to use the 'Human' class we created earlier to design a 'Batter' and a 'Bowler' class. A bowler is a human and inherits the human attributes, but in addition he or she has a batter who also inherits the human attributes.

```
class Bowler(Human):
      def __init__(self, initPos, initAge, initName,
initGen, bat):
            Human.__init__(self, initPos, initAge,
initName, initGen)
            self.batter = bat
            self.isBowler = True
            self.hasBatter = True
      def bowlAtBatter(self):
            self.batter.strikeBall()
            self.isBowler = None
            self.hasBatter = False
            print 'Bowler with name %s bowled at %s' %
(self.name, self.batter.name)
```

And the 'Batter' class:

```
class Batter(Human):
```

```
      def __init__(self, initPos, initAge, initName, initGen):
            Human.__init__(self, initPos, initAge,
initName, initGen)
            self.isBatter = True
      def strike(self):
            print 'Batter with name %s hit the ball.' %
(self.name)
```

Both the bowler and the batter are humans, but their interaction with each other is very different. The bowler bowls the ball at the batter, but the batter strikes the ball with his bat. They both inherit many common attributes from the 'Human' class, but their role-specific behaviour is added later as methods within their classes.

Each of the two classes inherits from the 'Human' class, denoted by the 'Human' object (the notes in the brackets to the right of the class name in the above example). In addition, a *constructor* (see above) is required to accommodate this inheritance by constructing a human object with the correct initialisation (line three of each class). Classes that are inherited from a parent class, are called *children* or *subclasses* of the parent class.

The methods 'bowlAtBatter' and 'strike' are added to the 'Bowler' and 'Batter' classes respectively since they are additional models of behaviour that are specific to the classes they are in.

Let's examine the difference between a 'Batter' and a 'Bowler':

```
andysPosition = Position(8, 1)
batterAndy = Batter( andysPosition , 34, 'Andy', 'male')
batterAndy .printDetails()
johnsPosition = Position(2, 21)
bowlerJohn = Manager(johnsPosition, 51, 'John', 'male',
  batterAndy )
bowlerJohn .printDetails()
```

```
$ Andy's age is 34 and is male.
$ He is at position (8, 1)
```

```
$ John's age is 51 and is male.
$ He is at position (2, 21)
```

Since both a 'Bowler' and a 'Batter' inherit attributes from 'Human', they can use all the same attributes and methods that 'Dave' was given previously.

```
print bowlerAndy.isBowler
print batterJohn.isBatter
bowlerAndy.bowlAtBatter()
$ True
$ True
$ Bowler with name Andy bowled at John
$ Batter with name John hit the ball
```

Because 'isBowler is an attribute added to a 'Bowler', we can get its value from any 'Bowler' object, and since 'isBatter is an attribute of a 'Batter', we can get its value for the object 'batterJohn'.

Likewise the method 'bowlAtBatter' is available to a 'Bowler'. Since we passed the object 'batterAndy' into the constructor of the 'Bowler', we now have access to her or his attributes and methods. Inside the 'bowlAtBatter' method of the 'Bowler' class, the 'strike' method of the 'Batter' is executed which models a batter striking the ball.

You should have now grasped the basic ideas behind OOP including attributes, methods, constructors and inheritance. You're not expected to be fully competent after having read this chapter, but my intention is that you've understood — at least in part — some of these difficult concepts.

Questions

1. How would you describe the difference between a class and an object?
2. What is OOP?
3. What is the role of a method of a class?
4. What is inheritance?

Chapter 6

The Graphical User Interface

We have been considering examples of computer programs that are entirely command-line based. That is, we have been inputting and outputting data to and from the command-line. But when we hear about a new piece of software that's been released, we are usually hearing about such things as a new social media website, a Microsoft Office upgrade or a new app for our smartphones, which seem to be very different to what we've covered so far.

Most software just appears to work like magic with windows appearing all over the place, impressive graphics, smooth transition animations, internet connectivity and many more features which do not seem like simply sets of computer instructions.

We must remember, however, that this is all that any program is — a set of instructions. There is no mystery behind real-time computer generated graphics or the World Wide Web (WWW). The programmers who developed *Call of Duty* and Google Chrome did so by using programming languages that use the same principles as we've been considering in this book. In fact, many of the features of our favourite websites use Python! Such is the power of 'abstraction'.

The control and manipulation of individual pixels on a computer screen is a low-level capability, but using software, we can build abstraction upon abstraction to generate classes which, for instance, can model 3D objects on our displays in real-time. And, using abstraction, we can write classes which take a basic binary signal between two computers and create applications which run across the Internet.

There is no magic involved in creating future groundbreaking applications. It can be done by anyone. As we go through the next three chapters, you will be amazed at just how easy it is to implement your genius ideas, no matter what they are.

wxPython

wxPython is a library for Python which abstracts away the complexities of generating classes for drawing Graphical User Interfaces (GUIs) — the windows which surround a desktop application such as Internet Explorer or Microsoft Word — onto the screen of a computer. wxPython makes creating these windows, including their menus, tabs, buttons, sliders, grids, combo-boxes and more, trivial. It is, moreover, *cross-platform*, which means that it runs on Windows, Mac and Linux computers.

We're going to start with a very simple example which displays a basic window to the screen.

```
#!/usr/bin/python
import wx
app = wx.App()
frame = wx.Frame(None, -1, 'First wxPython Window')
frame.Show()
app.MainLoop()
```

Much of this will look entirely unfamiliar to you so let us go through it line by line. The first line is the path to the Python interpreter that we have to include at the beginning of every program we write if we want to execute it without parsing it into the Python interpreter manually (mentioned in Chapter 2). The keyword 'import' in line two tells the Python interpreter that we want to use the wxPython toolkit, and so the interpreter then finds all of the classes that we may need to use. Then, in line three, we create a wxPython 'App' object which is an abstract object to store an instance of a wxPython application. Next, we create a 'Frame' object, which is an instantiation of the class which creates the outermost window of our application. The three parameters to its constructor are the frame's parent, which doesn't exist; an identifier which we've set to –1 and the title of the frame. This frame is a parent of other widgets (a component of an application) but does not have a parent itself.

We've then, in line five, executed the 'Show' method, to actually show our frame object on the screen. Line six enters the applications main loop, which then endlessly catches and dispatches *events* that exist during the life span of our application.

Despite this being a very simple example we can do a lot with this window. We can, for instance, move it, re-size it, minimize it or close it entirely. All this functionality would normally require a huge amount of coding, but this is already provided by wxPython.

Every individual item that can be placed inside a *wx.Frame* is known as a widget. These are children to the 'top-level' widget, which is usually a *wx.Frame*. (We can also use other top-level widgets including *wx.Dialog* or *wx.ScrolledWindow*.)

Inside our top-level widget, we can place the following:

- Containers, including
    - wx.ScrolledWindow
    - wx.Panel
    - wx.SplitterWindow
    - wx.Notebook
- Dynamic widgets, including
    - wx.ToggleButton
    - wx.CheckBox
    - wx.Button
    - wx.RadioButton
    - wx.ComboBox
    - etc.
- Static widgets, including
    - wx.StaticBox
    - wx.StaticText
    - wx.Gauge
- Other widgets, including
    - wx.Toolbar
    - wx.MenuBar
    - wx.StatusBar

'Containers' are widgets used as children of the top-level widget, and they 'contain' other widgets and arrange them in the required format. 'Dynamic' widgets are interactive and can be clicked, checked, toggled or selected, depending on what they are. 'Static' widgets hold content and stay in one place.

The three other widgets are the most important and don't fit into the other categories. wx.Toolbar and wx.MenuBar contain ordered 'buttons' that can be programmed to execute specific functions when clicked. The *wx.StatusBar* widget it typically found at the bottom of a window and displays information to the user to help them understand what is going on inside the window at any given time.

I am not telling you about these widgets on the assumpition that you'll be able to use them straight away, but to give you an idea of what's out there for you to use to create your GUIs. We would not cover them all, but we'll try out a few and hopefully that will give you the confidence to use other resources to find the specific widgets that you'll need in the future.

The Menu Bar and Buttons

A menu bar in wxPython is an object which can be created by calling `wx.MenuBar()` which is the constructor for the 'MenuBar' object in the 'wx' package. Below we have a complete wxPython application demonstrating a range of features in wxPython, including the menu bar, an item in the menu bar, a button and a dialogue window.

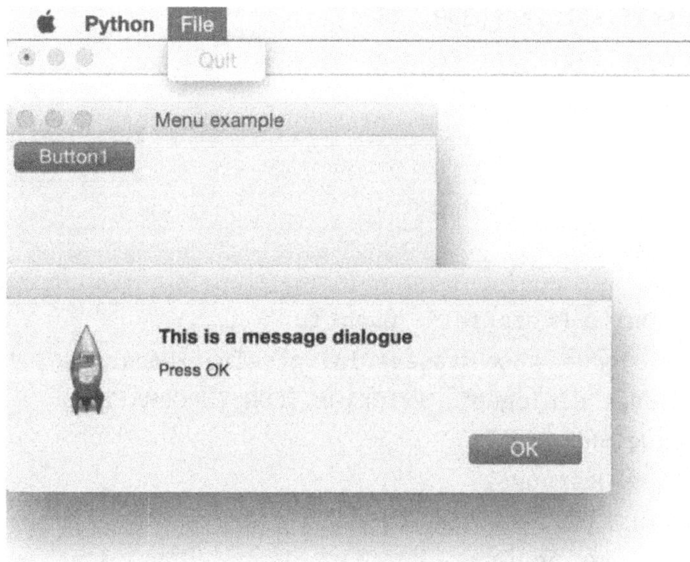

I will give you a step-by-step overview of what we're doing here as illustrated by the code below. We'll go through it in the order in which it gets executed, so we can see the process taking place.

```
#!/usr/bin/python
import wx
class MyMenu(wx.Frame):
  def __init__(self):
      super(MyMenu, self).__init__()
      menubar = wx.MenuBar()
      fileMenu = wx.Menu()
      fileMenu.Append(1, 'Quit', 'Quit application')
      menubar.Append(fileMenu, '&File')
      self.SetMenuBar(menubar)
      panel = wx.Panel(self, -1)
      wx.Button(panel, 2, "Button1", (0,0))
      wx.EVT_MENU(self, 1, self.OnQuit)
      wx.EVT_BUTTON(self, 2, self.OnButtonPress)
      self.SetSize((300, 200))
      self.SetTitle('Menu example')
      self.Centre()
      self.Show(True)

  def OnQuit(self, event):
      self.Close()

  def OnButtonPress(self, event):
      dialogue = wx.MessageDialog(self, 'Press OK', 'This
is a message dialogue', wx.OK|wx.ICON_INFORMATION)
  dialogue.ShowModal()
  dialogue.Destroy()
def main():
      ex = wx.App()
      MyMenu(None)
      ex.MainLoop()
```

```
if __name__ == '__main__':
    main()
```

The first thing to notice is that the last two lines in the code are:

```
if __name__ == '__main__':
    main()
```

You can think of this as simply causing the function 'main' to be executed when the Python interpreter runs your program. What's really happening 'under the hood' is that Python is setting its special internal variable '__name__' to the string '__main__', in order to execute the main part of the Python script it's been given.

Inside the 'main' function which Python executes next, our example wxPython 'App' object is instantiated and called 'ex':

```
def main():
    ex = wx.App()
    MyMenu(None)
    ex.MainLoop()
```

Next the class 'MyMenu' is instantiated and then enters its 'MainLoop' which causes it to begin its normal operating cycle. Obviously, it's inside 'MyMenu' that all the interesting stuff happens, so let's open up its constructor.

```
def __init__(self):
    super(MyMenu, self).__init__()
    menubar = wx.MenuBar()
    fileMenu = wx.Menu()
    fileMenu.Append(1, 'Quit', 'Quit application')
    menubar.Append(fileMenu, '&File')
    self.SetMenuBar(menubar)
    panel = wx.Panel(self, -1)
    wx.Button(panel, 2, "Button1", (0,0))
    wx.EVT_MENU(self, 1, self.OnQuit)
```

```
wx.EVT_BUTTON(self, 2, self.OnButtonPress)
self.SetSize((300, 200))
self.SetTitle('Menu example')
self.Centre()
self.Show(True)
```

Our menu bar inherits from the 'Frame' object, so we need to run the constructor of that object inside our own '__init__' function. The keyword 'super' in the above code denotes the class from which we're inheriting. The first line initializes this 'Frame' object and links it to our 'MyMenu' class.

Next we instantiate a 'MenuBar' object from the 'wx' library and name it 'menubar', and similarly instantiate a 'Menu' object called fileMenu. This is a child widget to the menu bar. A new item is added to this file menu using the 'Append' method. This method accepts three parameters: an identification number to later assign an action to it; a string of text to display on the button; and a description. The 'Append' method adds the file menu to the menu bar that we've named 'menubar'. Next, we call on the 'SetMenuBar' method which belongs to the 'wx.Frame' class that we've inherited from, and it sets up the menu bar in our frame.

```
panel = wx.Panel(self, -1)
wx.Button(panel, 2, "Button1", (0,0))
wx.EVT_MENU(self, 1, self.OnQuit)
wx.EVT_BUTTON(self, 2, self.OnButtonPress)
```

We then create a 'wx.Panel' object which will be a container for our button. We instantiate a 'wx.Button' object, place it inside 'panel', assign it an identification number, a name and a position inside the container, as required by the parameters of the button's constructor.

The last two lines of the code in the box above set up what are known as 'event listeners'. These can be thought of as objects that execute a function when an event occurs, such as the pressing of a button or the moving of a mouse. 'wx.EVT_MENU' is here used to setup a menu event listener where, in this case, we specify the widget with ID equal to 1 to execute the 'OnQuit' method that we're to define. We also use 'wx.EVT_BUTTON' to cause our button with ID equal to 2 to execute a command called by us 'OnButtonPress'. Both of these methods are specified in our MyMenu class and we'll take a look at them in a moment.

```
        self.SetSize((300, 200))
        self.SetTitle('Menu example')
        self.Centre()
        self.Show(True)
```

Finally, we set the *x*- and *y*-coordinates; the title and the position of our frame; and set its visibility state to be 'visible'. All of these methods are inherited from the 'wx.Frame' object.

As shown in the example code below, the 'OnQuit' method simply calls the 'Close' method inherited from the 'Frame' class which causes our 'MyMenu' object to close, that is:

```
def OnQuit(self, event):
        self.Close()
           dialogue.Destroy()
```

When our button is pressed, the 'OnButtonPress' method is executed as instructed. Then, the following three lines of code are executed:

```
def OnButtonPress(self, event):
        dialogue = wx.MessageDialog(self, 'Press OK', 'This
is a message dialogue', wx.OK|wx.ICON_INFORMATION)
        dialogue.ShowModal()
        dialogue.Destroy()
```

A built-in 'MessageDialog' object is created which displays a message. Its parameters are the calling class which is 'self', the instruction text 'Press OK' and the message to display — "This is a message dialogue”. These dialogues and others are useful for such tasks as notifying the user of something, requiring a confirmation from the user, acquiring a text-entry from the user and a range of other tasks.

The ‘ShowModal’ method shows the dialogue to the user. The word ‘modal’ indicates that the user cannot do anything with the application until they click ‘OK’ on the dialogue. When the user does click ‘OK’, this method returns and the dialogue is destroyed.

This brief introduction to wxPython should have served to highlight the ease with which graphical programs can be designed using Python, as well as giving you the motivation and confidence to discover more uses of wxPython and the range of widgets it provides.

Questions

1. What is wxPython, and what is it used for?
2. What is a wxPython widget, and what different widgets are available?
3. What method of the wx.Frame class is called to select the size of the Window to be displayed?
4. What is an ‘event’ in wxPython and how are they used? How would you specify that a certain function should be executed when a button is pressed, using an event?

Web Development

Chapter 7

Sockets, Networks and the World Wide Web

The Internet in the 21st century — social media, e-commerce, news and entertainment. Even our personal banking is now online. But this has not always been the case. The first computers only worked on one task at a time — a highly inefficient method which lacked the capability that users sought. They were large and needed storing in large cooled rooms which were far removed from whoever was using them.

In the late 1950s, a big change occurred in computing. A remote connection was established between computers which led to the idea that computers could be shared, allowing the processing power of one computer to be shared between multiple users.

In 1957 during the Cold War, the first unmanned satellite, Sputnik 1, was sent into orbit by the Soviet Union. The fear of a 'missile gap' emerged, and in order to secure America's lead in technology, the United States of America founded DARPA — the Defence Advanced Research Project Agency — in February 1958. DARPA planned a large scale computer network, in order to speed the transfer of knowledge and information. This network would later become the ARPANET. This, and the scientific, military and commercial advances of several other concepts from the US, France, and England, among others, formed the major foundations of our modern Internet.

Networks

The Internet is a global network of computers and other devices which communicate with each other and share data, but what exactly *is* a network? Well, a computer network is a collection of two or more computers linked by a shared connection. This means that they can interact with each other, via this connection. They can share data with each other, as well as resources such as printers, modems and data storage drives.

When networks at multiple locations are further connected to each other using, for instance, shared channels provided by phone companies, computers can send emails, share files and provide a range of services to remote users.

Every network includes at a minimum at least two computers, as well as network interface cards (NICs), a connection medium (usually a wire) and a networking operating system (OS), such as Windows, OS X or Linux.

Examples of these networks include:

Local Area Networks

Local area networks (LANs) are networks that are typically confined to a particular geographical area, such as a university, company or other organization. They can link as few as two computers together, but are typically comprised of many computers, used by many people. Standardised 'networking protocols' (rules governing the format of messages sent between networked computers) have led to the widespread use of LANs in business and educational organisations across the globe. In addition, wireless communication can be used, allowing devices with wireless capability to connect easily to a network. These are called Wireless LANs (WLANs).

Wide Area Networks (WANs)

'Wide area networking' connects multiple LANs that are geographically separated. This is accomplished by connecting the different

LANs by phone lines, satellite links, and/or data packet carrier services (broadband). Wide area networking can be as simple as one modem and a computer for remote users to connect to, or as complex as a network of hundreds of an organisation's branches connecting from all over the world.

The Internet

The Internet is a worldwide network of connected smaller networks, providing data communication services to those who request it. The World Wide Web (WWW) is considered synonymous with the Internet, and provides a network of global services such as remote login, file transfer, email and websites, which are accessible from any computer connected to the Internet.

With the massive increase in demand for connectivity, the Internet has become a digital highway for billions of users. Internet websites now provide social, educational, political and financial resources to every country on the planet.

Intranet

Similar to the Internet, an Intranet is a private network within an organisation which provides similar features as the Internet, but whose availability is limited to be only within that organisation. Intranets are most commonly used for providing easy access to corporate information within an organisation.

Whetever the type of network, they all use two types of computers. These are *clients* and *servers*. Physically these computers look similar, but their configuration and usage determines the role they have to play in a network. A *server* is a computer configured to provide some kind of service to other servers or clients within the network, such as file storage, printing services or other shared resources. A *client* is a computer in the network which connects with those servers, or with other clients, to access shared resources.

A client/server network is the most efficient way to provide

- Databases,
- Management of applications such as spreadsheets, accounting, communications and document managers,
- Network management,
- Shared file storage.

At the heart of this kind of network is the concept of splitting the function of applications between the server and client to let the most appropriate functions be completed by the right computer, to be shared with other users in the desired manner.

Networking in Python

As has already been alluded to, in order for a computer to be connected to a network it must be running an OS that can handle connections from other devices over a network. Thankfully, most modern OS support this functionality and Python enables the underlying capability of these OSs to let programmers connect clients and servers together over a network.

Python provides two levels of access to networked services. The most basic low-level networking capability is provided by *sockets.* These can be thought of as connections between computers that allow clients and servers to access a network. They are the endpoints of a bidirectional communications channel between two computers.

Python also contains *libraries* which provide higher level access to specific protocols operating over the Internet, including the hypertext transfer protocol (HTTP) which will be discussed later. The library contains classes for handling the communication of data between the two endpoints.

IP addresses and Ports

An Internet Protocol (IP) address is a numerical address assigned to every device in a network, in order to identify it. There is a huge amount to know about IP addresses and how they identify a device and then establish a connection to it, but here we're only concerned with the basics.

There are two primary types of IP address — IPv4 and IPv6 (versions 4 and 6). IPv4 is the original IP address format which is still most common. It is made up of a 32-bit or 4-byte number, separated into 4 parts.

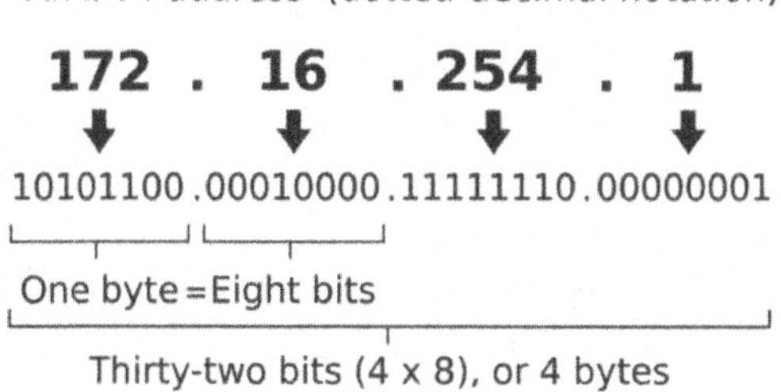

A *bit* is a single 1 or 0 that a computer can understand. A *byte* is a group of 8 bits, each of which can be set to a different value. The byte, although a binary number, has a decimal representation, as depicted in the image above. Each of the 4 bytes or decimal numbers which comprise an IPv4 address can range in their decimal representation from 0 to 255, and make up the unique identifier of the networked device.

IPv6 is the new format for IP addresses. It is a longer address, introduced as a result of the rapid exhaustion of the possible values of and IPv4 address which would eventually limit the number of devices able to connect to the Internet.

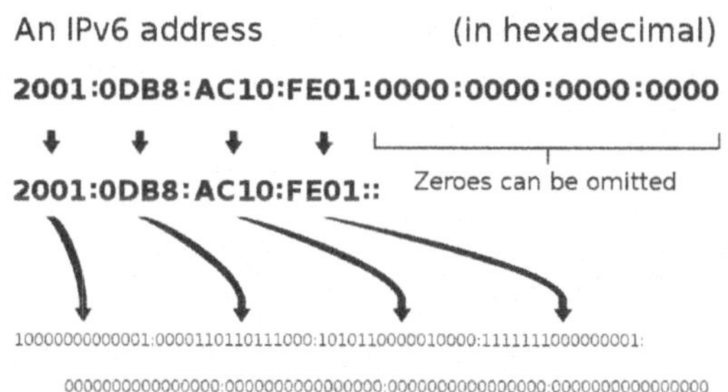

The illustration above shows an example of an IPv6 address which is made up of a far greater number of bits and, as a consequence, has a much larger range of possible values. This allows for a larger number of devices to be connected to a network, as there is a greater range of unique identifiers available.

In addition to IP addresses, the other important part of a connection between two computers is the *port*. A computer can be connected to multiple servers at once and transmit data to some or all of them simultaneously! It can, for instance, be printing a file using one server on a LAN at the same time as receiving a web page from a server on the Internet. Clearly this requires two separate connections — one between the client and the printing server, and one between the client and the web server on the Internet. As the client only has one single unique IP address, another way is needed to provide a distinction between the two connections and prevent them from interfering with each other. This is where ports come in.

Think of a port. Yes, a real world port. As in a port that ships come into. These ports are in a single location, like Southampton, New York or Sydney, and these ports have a single address that every ship heads to when it needs to deliver goods. But this doesn't mean that only one ship at a time can use the port — rather there are multiple berths at the same port that different ships can use to unload their cargo.

A port on a computer, is a bit like a berth at a real port and allows for multiple simultaneous connections to different devices.

Port numbers are numbered for consistency and ease of use for programmers. Typically ports 0 to 1023 are dedicated for use by the Internet, but in practice almost any port can be used for any service.

All of this means that when making a connection from one computer to another, we'll need to specify both an IP address to connect to and a port number.

TCP and UDP

When any channel of communication is established, both the sender and the recipient must agree on a protocol to use before beginning communication. Think of sending or receiving a letter. A written or spoken language is being used, and each word we say is received and interpreted by the recipient. To ensure the letter is delivered, we need to specify their address on the envelope so that the postal service knows where to deliver it. We also write our own address on the back, so that the recipient can respond to our letter if required.

When a computer transmits data, it is sent as tiny *packets* of information, like sending a letter. As well as the information, these packets contain a set of 'meta-data' or 'headers' which includes the IP address of the destination computer. These headers instruct the network where and how to deliver the packet.

There are two primary protocols used by computers to transmit data between them. These protocols are 'TCP' and 'UDP', with TCP standing for *Transmission Control Protocol* and UDP standing for *User Datagram Protocol.* They each use slightly different means of delivering packets to each other and each has its benefits and drawbacks.

TCP is a more reliable, connection-based protocol for transmitting data. It requires two available anchored end-points, defining the connection between the sending location and the receiving location. Using TCP, data always arrives in the order that it was sent, and is only ever lost if the connection is broken. A TCP connection can be broken if either end-point loses connection to the Internet.

UDP is a connectionless protocol. This means that data is sent regardless of whether or not the computer at the destination IP address is available, existent or listening. Unfortunately, using UDP there is no guarantee that the data will ever be received. However when UDP works it is a much faster method of transmitting data. The UDP protocol, therefore, is particularly good for transmitting packets containing parts of media files, such as steaming videos, where it doesn't necessarily matter whether or not a particular packet is received or not.

Simple Client/Server Example

A socket is capable of establishing a connection not only across the world, but also from one computer back to itself. In order that we do not need to setup two computers to talk to each other, we are going to design two programs which talk to each other on the same computer. The principle for talking between two or more separate computers is exactly the same, except we would need to know the separate IP addresses of the computers involved.

First off, we have got a program to act as a server. This program will create a socket and start listening on port 8089 for a client to connect to it. When a client is connected, it will send a message to the client and establish the connection.

```
#!/usr/bin/python
# Example server program called server.py

import socket          # Import socket module
mySocket = socket.socket() # Create a socket object
host = socket.gethostname() # Get local machine name
port = 8089            # Reserve a port for your service.
mySocket.bind((host, port))  # Bind to the port
mySocket.listen(5)         # Now wait for client connection.
while True:
       connection, addr = mySocket.accept() # Establish
           connection
       print 'Got connection from ' + addr
       connection.send('Thank you for connecting')
       connection.close()        # Close the connection
```

In the two lines of the example program of the server above, we first import the Python socket library and create a socket object by calling the constructor of the 'socket' class within the socket's library. We then find the name of the local machine (host) and *bind* the socket to this port using the 'bind' method of the socket, which we've called 'mySocket'. The host in this example can be considered synonymous with the IP address. The socket's 'listen' method — which listens on our port for connections and returns when a connection is made — is then called. We've set the number of maximum connections that can be made to five by specifying this in the parameter for the 'listen' method of our socket, 'mySocket.listen(5)'.

Lastly, our server enters an infinite loop, which never ends because the condition of the 'while' loop is always true. In a real-world implementation of a server-side program, this would be replaced with the specific functionality offered by the server. When the connection is established by accepting the connection request, both the 'connection' object and the address of the client are stored. Both of these objects are then returned when the 'accept' method of the socket is called. A message is sent using a TCP packet to the client using the 'send' method of the connection and finally the connection is closed before the loop is repeated.

The example client program below is simpler and must be executed after the server program as, if the client program is executed first, the port on the server will not be listening for the connection and we will not be able to establish one.

```
#!/usr/bin/python
# Example client program called client.py

import socket # Import socket module

mySocket = socket.socket() # Create a socket object
host = socket.gethostname() # Get local machine name
port = 8089 # Reserve a port for your service.
mySocket.connect((host, port))
print mySocket.recv(1024)
mySocket.close # Close the socket when done
```

The client program similarly instantiates a 'socket' object. Since the client is connecting to the same host as the server, namely itself, it can use the 'gethostname' method, which also returns the IP address of the local machine. Every network-enabled device has a 'host' commonly referred to as the *localhost*. We connect to the same port that the server is bound to, and therefore listening on, and attempt to make a connection using the 'connect' method on the socket. The 'recv' method of our socket recognises when a message is received from the server, and the return value is then printed on the screen, after which the connection is closed.

We first run our server in the background, by appending the usual command with an ampersand (&). We then run our client program and observe our output.

```
# The following starts a server in the background
$ python server.py &

# Once server is started, we run the client
$ python client.py
```

In this case, our output is as follows:

```
$ Got connection from ('localhost', 8089)
 Thank you for connecting
```

We can infer from this output that the server is correctly set up and bound to port 8089 on the localhost. We can also infer that the client connected correctly to the same port, and received appropriate message sent from the server.

This basic idea forms the basis of all networked applications, by providing a connection between computers through which information can be shared. A socket is a very primitive and low-level layer of abstraction connecting peers on a network, yet it forms the foundation upon which higher-level networked applications interact with each other.

Questions

1. What do the acronyms LAN and WLAN stand for, and what is the difference between them?
2. What are IP addresses and ports?
3. What is the difference between TCP and UDP as protocols for sending information across the Internet?
4. What is a socket?

Chapter 8

HTML, CSS and JavaScript

Just by glancing at the title of this chapter, you may well have seen a bunch of names or acronyms you know nothing about, so I'm going to tell you about another one, just to get you well and truly confuzzled. *HTTP* stands for *HyperText Transfer Protocol*, which means that it is a protocol for transferring HyperText. HyperText is, in essence, regular text with 'links' in it, where a 'link' is a shortcut to another web page. HTTP is the protocol you use every time you load a web page on the Internet. It is specified by the little 'http://' which comes before the 'www' in a website's address, which tells your browser that you are using the HTTP protocol to access the web page.

We can use HTTP to get information from just about anywhere on the Internet, and this information comes from *servers*. The Internet is full of clients like you and me, who ask for various resources. These resources include files, web pages, videos, pictures, applications and other forms of data, and they are all stored on various servers. When you make a 'HTTP request', you are burning through the network until a server is found that is able to respond to the request. When it finds that server, the server responds to you with a 'HTTP response'. A HTTP request is called a 'GET' request and a HTTP response is called a 'POST' request. A GET request seeks a resource from a server using HTTP, and a POST request seeks to deliver that resource using HTTP.

HTML

Most desktop applications read and write files in a particular format. Microsoft Excel can handle .xlsx or .xls files. PowerPoint can handle .pptx or .ppt files. These files are nothing special, but are merely a set of instructions on how to rebuild the objects contained in the files the next time they are opened in a compatible program. It is exactly the same for internet applications.

HTML stands for *HyperText Markup Language* and is used to describe the contents of a web page, and how it should be displayed. It is a language which is understood by a browser and allows content to be sent as text over a network such as the Internet and displayed as required. It's just a textual representation of content and how that content should be shown by the browser receiving it.

The structure of a HTML page is fairly consistent, so it will be beneficial for you to become familiar with the example below, which is the code describing a very basic page.

```
<!DOCTYPE html>
<html>
  <head>
    <title>Title of page</title>
  </head>
  <body>
    <h1>My First Heading</h1>
    <p>My first paragraph</p>
    <h2>My First Sub-heading</h2>
    <p>My second paragraph</p>
  </body>
</html>
```

The first thing you'll notice is that there are lots of angle brackets (< and >) throughout, with keywords in the middle. The "<some_text>" part is called a 'tag', and is used to denote the start of a particular section of content. This opening tag is accompanied by a complementary "</some_text>" which closes the section of content.

There is a line in the above example which uses the <title> tag shown below. This is a tag which tells the browser that the text in the middle of the <title> tag is the title of the web page. In our case, we want the title of the page to be the string 'Title of page'. The contents of tags are often referred to as *elements.*

```
<title>Title of page</title>
```

You'll have seen from out page outline that a tag can contain other tags within it. For example the <html> tag is a tag which denotes the start and end of the contents of the HTML page. Inside the HTML element are contained a pair of <head> tags and <body> tags which appear consecutively. The <head> element of a HTML page contains the <title> element and can contain a range of additional meta-data related to the behaviour of the page.

The <body> element contains the primary content of the page including headers, sub-headers, paragraphs, images, links and much more. In our example we've included a header ('<h1> </h1>') followed by a paragraph ('<p> </p>') and a sub-heading ('<h2> </h2>') followed by another paragraph.

You can view a HTML document by saving the HTML to a text file with the .html file type and dragging the file into your browser.

As you can see from the screenshot above, this basic page is extremely plain and contains no interesting colours, fonts, or styling

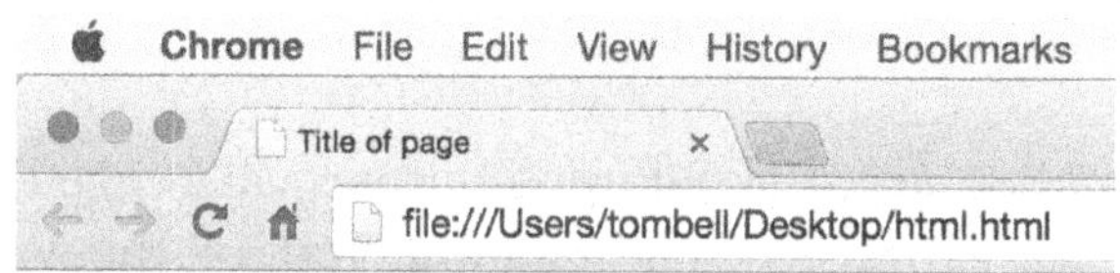

whatsoever. This is something that we solve using what is called 'Cascading Style Sheets' or CSS.

CSS

Cascading Style Sheets (CSSs) is a language for specifying how HTML pages should be displayed to users. Take the example below — a modified version of our previous example. Here, we've placed a paragraph element within our main body, and have encapsulated the first letter of each word inside a pair of <strong> tags. A <strong> tag is a tag built in to HTML which gives a stronger font to the next element contained within the tag.

```
<!DOCTYPE html>
<html>
  <head>
    <title>Sample document</title>
  </head>
  <body>
    <p>
     <strong>C</strong>ascading
     <strong>S</strong>tyle
     <strong>S</strong>heets
    </p>
  </body>
</html>
```

You should observe the following output, where the first letter of each word has a heavier font than the rest of the word, as we specified.

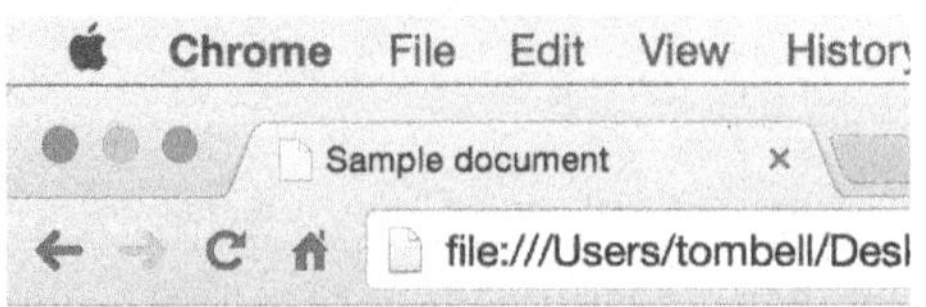

Cascading Style Sheets

(Due to your specific browser, this may not necessarily appear exactly the same as the screenshot above, but the differences are not important.)

At present we are not using any CSS at all, but we can include CSS to define a style for our web page, including the design, layout and variations for different display sizes.

Here is our first cascading style sheet, saved as a file called style.css:

```
strong {color: red;}
```

This says that for <strong> tags, the colour is set to red. This same syntax can be applied to different tags and can be used to set a range of display options. Now, we modify our HTML to link it to the CSS file.

```
<!DOCTYPE html>
<html>
 <head>
   <title>Sample document</title>
   <link rel="stylesheet" href="style.css">
 </head>
 <body>
   <p>
    <strong>C</strong>ascading
    <strong>S</strong>tyle
    <strong>S</strong>heets
   </p>
 </body>
</html>
```

As you may have guessed, this causes the letters enclosed in the <strong> tag to be not only bolder, but also red.

The '<link>' element in the example above contains two *attributes* which provide additional information about HTML elements. A <link> element links a HTML page to an external style sheet (ESS). The attribute 'rel' stands for 'relationship' and specifies the relationship between the current document and the linked document. 'href' stands for hyperlink reference and contains the relative path to the CSS file to be linked the current document.

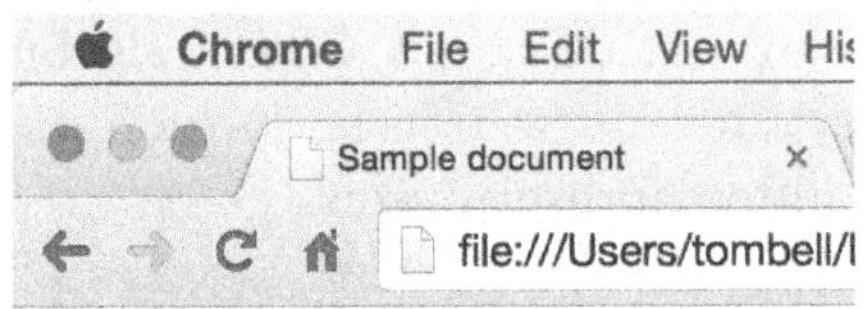

The following example uses the original modification of the <strong> element, but also affects paragraph tags (<p>). We've added two stylistic features to the paragraphs — we've changed the colour to blue, and indicated that the text-decoration be underlined.

```
strong {
        color: red;
}
p {
        color: blue;
        text-decoration: underline;
}
```

Since we've now got a more complex style sheet, we've properly indented our CSS file to be more readable.

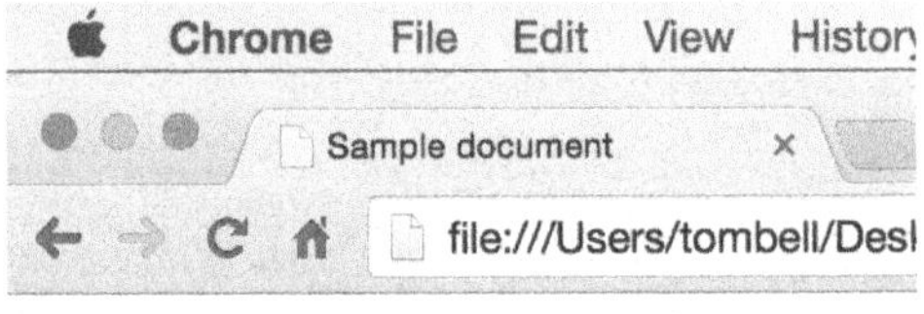

You may have noticed that the text inside the <strong> tag is also inside the <p> tag and that there are different text colour specifications for each — in the <p> tag the text is blue, but in the <strong> tag it is red. In this case, since the <strong> tag is inside the <p> tag, it is the last tag to affect the contents of that element, so the style for the <strong> tag takes precedence.

The final thing we need to be introduced to is the most powerful and important HTML element. It's called the '<div>' tag which stands for a division. We're going to take a look at it here because it's only relevant when using CSS. It's a tag used to separate one piece of content from another. Completely controllable using CSS, <div> tags are highly flexible in terms of their position, behaviour (as, for instance, when the page resizes) and their content.

```
<!DOCTYPE html>
<html>
<body>
	<h1>This is a heading</h1>
	<div>
	First div tag contents. First div tag contents. First div tag contents. First div tag contents. First div tag contents. First div tag contents. First div tag contents. First div tag contents. First div tag contents. First div tag contents. First div tag contents. First div tag contents. First div tag contents. First div tag contents. First div tag contents.
	</div>
	<div>
	Second div tag contents. Second div tag contents. Second div tag contents. Second div tag contents. Second div tag contents. Second div tag contents. Second div tag contents. Second div tag contents. Second div tag contents. Second div tag contents. Second div tag contents. Second div tag contents. Second div tag contents. Second div tag contents. Second div tag contents.
	</div>
</body>
</html>
```

The code in the previous page illustrates the use of two <div> tags. As you can see from the screenshot below, the default behaviour of a <div> tag is to contain its content (text in this case) in a vertical order, similar to the <p> (paragraph) element.

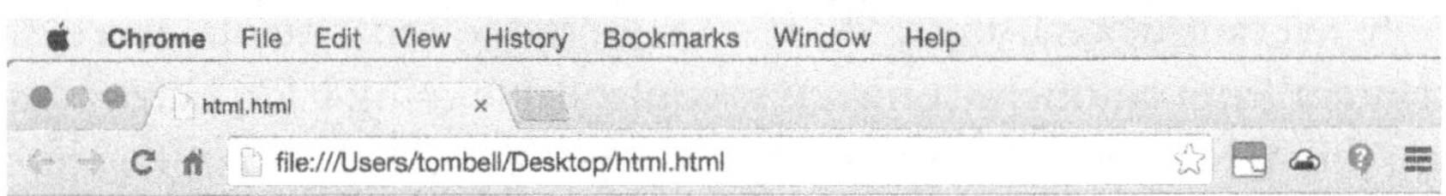
Chrome File Edit View History Bookmarks Window Help
html.html
file:///Users/tombell/Desktop/html.html
This is a heading
First div tag contents. First div tag contents. First div tag contents. First div tag contents. First div tag contents. First div tag contents. First div tag contents. First div tag contents. First div tag contents. First div tag contents. First div tag contents. First div tag contents. First div tag contents. First div tag contents. First div tag contents.
Second div tag contents. Second div tag contents. Second div tag contents. Second div tag contents. Second div tag contents. Second div tag contents. Second div tag contents. Second div tag contents. Second div tag contents. Second div tag contents. Second div tag contents. Second div tag contents. Second div tag contents. Second div tag contents. Second div tag contents.

The above example uses <div> tags with no style formatting whatsoever. However the primary purpose of <div> tags is their ability to be used to specify the style behaviour of a part of a web page.

The example below is a HTML page containing a selection of <div> tags which shows this clearly. We've surrounded our content in a <div> tag with 'id' attributes set, where an 'id' attribute is a way to identify a particular tag, using CSS to provide it with custom styles. We've surrounded both the header, the content and the footer of this example page with <div> tags and have used appropriate 'id' values for each.

```
<!DOCTYPE html>
<html>
<head>
  <title>Sample document</title>
  <link rel=“stylesheet” href=“style.css”>
  </head>
<body>
<div id=“container”>
      <div id=“header”>
            <h1>Web page Title</h1>
```

```
        </div>
        <div id="content">
                <div>
                First div tag contents. First div tag contents.
First div tag contents. First div tag contents. First div tag
contents. First div tag contents. First div tag contents.
First div tag contents. First div tag contents. First div tag
contents. First div tag contents. First div tag contents.
First div tag contents. First div tag contents. First div
tag contents.
                </div>
                <div>
                Second div tag contents. Second div tag
contents. Second div tag contents. Second div tag contents.
Second div tag contents. Second div tag contents. Second
div tag contents. Second div tag contents. Second div tag
contents. Second div tag contents. Second div tag contents.
Second div tag contents. Second div tag contents. Second div
tag contents.
                </div>
        </div>
        <div id="footer">
        Footer of div tag example
        </div>
</div>
</body>
</html>
```

The CSS file 'style.css' is shown next and is used to complement this HTML page. In CSS, the elements of a page with an ID set (denoted by the 'id' attribute) are accessed using a # symbol followed by the value of the ID. Within the block inside the curly brackets, we can then specify the style to be applied to the elements that have been accessed using that ID.

```
h1 {
      margin-bottom:10;
}
#header {
      background-color:#BFF006;
}
#content {
      border:1px solid green;
      text-align:left;
}
#footer {
      background-color:#BFF006;
      clear:both;
      text-align:center;
}
```

The screenshot below illustrates what the output of this page looks like. We've set the background colour of the element with ID 'header' and 'footer' to be green and the border of the element with ID 'content' to be one pixel wide, and to also be green.

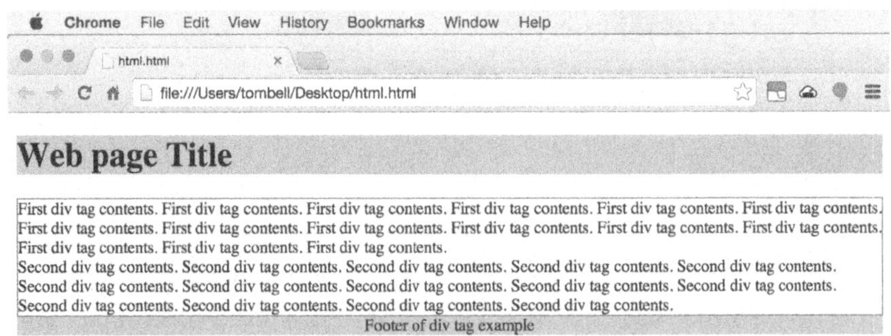
Chrome File Edit View History Bookmarks Window Help
html.html
file:///Users/tombell/Desktop/html.html
Web page Title
First div tag contents. First div tag contents. First div tag contents. First div tag contents. First div tag contents. First div tag contents.
First div tag contents. First div tag contents. First div tag contents. First div tag contents. First div tag contents. First div tag contents.
First div tag contents. First div tag contents. First div tag contents.
Second div tag contents. Second div tag contents. Second div tag contents. Second div tag contents. Second div tag contents.
Second div tag contents. Second div tag contents. Second div tag contents. Second div tag contents. Second div tag contents.
Second div tag contents. Second div tag contents. Second div tag contents. Second div tag contents.
Footer of div tag example

As you can see from the CSS above, the text alignment of the text within the content has been set to 'left' whereas the footer text alignment is centred. The 'margin-bottom' style attribute given to the 'h1' tag denotes that a blank margin of size 10 should be added to the bottom of every header. This can be seen as the blank space underneath the header in the page screenshot in the previous page.

As can be seen, <div> tags are immensely powerful for a host of reasons and the vast majority of modern web pages are based on the interaction of CSS with <div> tags in HTML.

JavaScript

We have all used some pretty fancy web applications as web technology has progressed, whether Netflix to watch movies or Facebook with awesome features like chat and notification. While we've been introduced to HTML and CSS already (both of which are used by these popular web applications) you may suspect that something more is required for much of the behaviour demonstrated by these sites. That something is JavaScript.

One of the brilliant things about using JavaScript it that is requires almost no setting up to be able to develop and test your own JavaScript code. All you need is a text editor, and a web browser like Google Chrome or Mozilla Firefox. To try out the following examples, you can simply copy them into your own .html file, and then test them instantly simply by dragging the file into your browser.

JavaScript is a language that is used to add behaviour to the 'front-end' of a web application. The term front-end, refers to the client's computer as opposed to the server hosting the website. Thus, JavaScript is an interpreted language that is sent to the client when a page is requested from the web server. When it arrives at the client, the client's browser executes the JavaScript code and some operation is performed.

JavaScript code can also be executed when a user interacts with a page, such as at the touch of a button or mouse move. It can be used, for instance, to validate a user's input into a text field, to provide drag and drop functionality, to change the style of the web page on-the-fly, to animate parts of the page and even to deliver rich graphics that the user can interact with.

All this functionality revolves around the idea of *event handling*. This is a concept that's not unique to JavaScript, but which is fundamental to understanding how it works. Almost every piece of JavaScript is triggered as a result of an *event*. Events can be page loads, button clicks, mouse moves, double clicks or mouse drags, and a multitude of other things.

The specifics of event handling are far too extensive to be covered in this chapter, but we'll use the next few pages to go through a couple of examples to demonstrate some different ways to include JavaScript in a web page and a selection of things you can do with it.

In the sample code below, all we've got is a paragraph element <p>. The paragraph element has an attribute 'onclick', which is an *event listener* which listens for a 'click' event. The value assigned to the 'onclick' attribute is a string containing JavaScript code.

```
<p onclick="alert('Hello World!');">Click Here</p>
```

This example can be inserted into our original basic HTML page in the <body> element, or can be used as a stand alone HTML document. When we open it in our browser and click the text in the paragraph, an alert dialogue appears displaying the text 'Hello World!', as shown below.

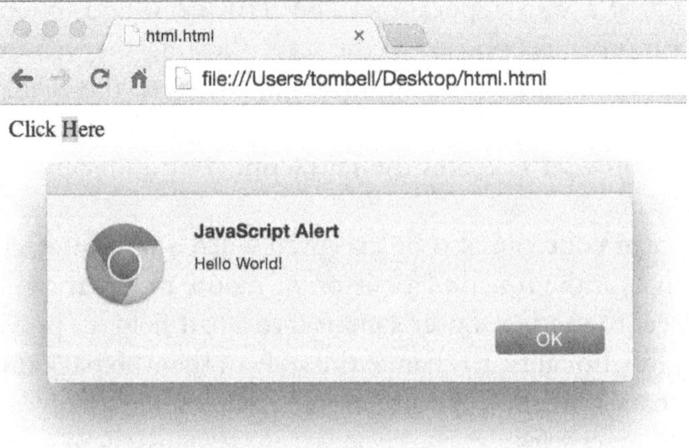

The JavaScript code executes the built-in JavaScript function 'alert' which produces this dialogue. The parameter of this method is the string of text to display. Alert dialogues can be used in a range of situations on a web page, but for now, we're only using it to illustrate how events work.

Of course the ability to produce a basic message box is nothing exciting, so what about if we wanted to do something more interesting with the same event? Let us look at a more complex example. Instead of calling JavaScript's built-in dialogue function directly, we can call our own function.

```
<script>
 function clickHandler() {
  alert("Hello, World!");
 }
</script>
<p onclick="clickHandler();">Click Here</p>
```

In this example, we've used the HTML <script> element. Within the <script> tags, we can define our very own JavaScript function from scratch, right within our HTML page. When our paragraph is clicked, JavaScript will resolve the 'onclick' event handler to execute our own function 'clickHandler' that we've defined already. This produces exactly the same result as before.

It is probably worth noting here that as with most programming languages, the syntax of JavaScript varies somewhat from Python. In Python we used indentation to denote the start of a method. In JavaScript, a *function* (effectively a method) is denoted by curly brackets '{}', as can be seen in the example above. Instead of 'def' as used in Python, in JavaScript the keyword 'function' is used to denote the start of a function, and is always followed by the name of the function. Parameters are specified in the brackets, and the individual instructions within the function are specified in the curly brackets.

We can also incorporate JavaScript from an external file using two attributes inside the opening <script> tag.

```
<script type="text/javascript" src="scriptName.js"></script>
```

The ‘type’ attribute denotes that we are including text containing JavaScript code, and the ‘src’ (source) attribute specifies the path to the file which contains the JavaScript we wish to include.

We can perform complex mathematics in JavaScript, which can be explained using simple examples. In the example below, for instance, we’ve specified three elements within our <body> tag. These are a blank paragraph element with the ‘id’ attribute set to ‘demo’; a <script> element with a function defined; and our original button with an ‘onclick’ event listener.

```
<!DOCTYPE html>
<html>
 <body>
  <p id="demo"></p>
       <script>
         function myFunction() {
         var x = 2;
         var y = 3;
         document.getElementById("demo").innerHTML = x + y;
       }
      </script>
  <p onclick="myFunction();">Click Here</p>
 </body>
</html>
```

The ‘id’ attribute is an identifier for that element which can be used in a number of ways to affect that element as well as the format of its contents. The JavaScript keyword ‘var’ denotes the declaration of a variable. In our function ‘myFunction’, we’ve defined two variables which are assigned the numbers 2 and 3. The third line inside this function is where the action happens. In words, we are resolving the sum of *x* and *y* and assigning the result to the inner HTML of the element with the ID ‘demo’. The JavaScript engine within your browser is actually doing the following — taking the built-in

JavaScript object 'document' which is your web page; using its 'getElementById' method which returns the object representing the element with the ID passed into that method; getting the instance variable 'innerHTML' of that element which is the text inside the element's tags; and setting it to the string conversion of the numerical sum of the variables *x* and *y*. Here's the page that you will see once the 'Click Here' text is pressed:

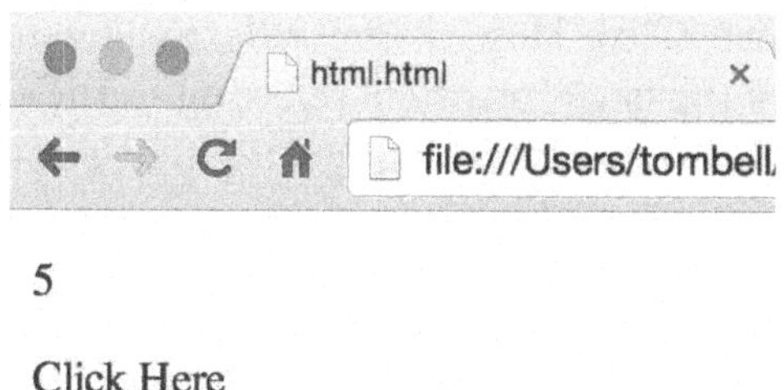

This ability of JavaScript is a hugely powerful feature, because it enables web developers to change the contents of their web pages after they have already been loaded.

In addition to creating dialogues and performing calculations, JavaScript is perfect for the graphical manipulation of websites. It is used to move elements around, change their sizes and orientations, and even replace old content with new content. In the final example page below, we've modified our function to get the paragraph element <p> with the ID 'demo' and change the colour of the text inside it to green.

```
<!DOCTYPE html>
<html>
 <body>
      <script>
        function myFunction() {
             document.getElementById(“demo”).style.color =
‘green’;
        }
```

```
      </script>
      <p id="demo>
       This is a test.
      </p>
  <p onclick="myFunction();">Click Here</p>
 </body>
</html>
```

When the text 'Click Here' is pressed, 'myFunction' is executed and the 'color' of the 'style' attribute referring to the element with ID 'demo' is changed to 'green' which sets the font's colour to green.

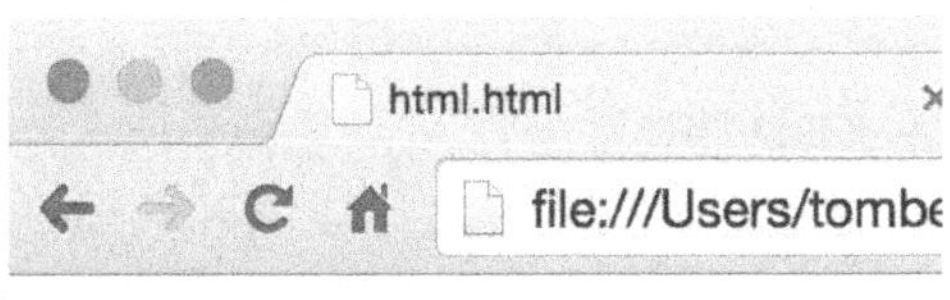

This is a test.

Click Here

The image above illustrates the contents of this page when the 'onclick' event is handled by our function.

This combination of HTML, CSS and JavaScript forms the basis of the vast majority of front-end websites. There are a whole host of different functions that we've not covered in this brief introduction, however what we have covered should have provided you with enough understanding to get the general gist of how web pages work, and given you the confidence to investigate for yourselves what more can be done to make the user-facing side of your websites full-featured works of art.

Questions

1. What are the two pieces of information needed for a client to connect to a server using a socket?

2. What does HTML stand for and what is it used for?
3. Which language does a stylesheet use to manage how a HTML page appears on a device?
4. What is CSS used for and how can it be used to change the colour of a paragraph element in HTML?
5. How is a JavaScript function executed from within a HTML web page?
6. Which JavaScript function is used to display a popup box to the user?

Chapter 9
PHP and SQL

When you walk into an up-market restaurant for your favourite cuisine, you will no doubt be greeted by your waiter or waitress with a welcoming smile and guided to a comfortable chair in pleasant surroundings. That is because customer service in restaurants is of upmost importance for retaining consumers by giving them the incentive to come back. While there may be a host of chefs in the kitchen preparing your dinner and getting their hands dirty, you are kept blissfully unaware of what background stresses, hard work and skills may be required to make your relaxing evening happen.

In the development of web applications the same principles are applied. The important functions — often large and complex — are performed for you automatically on the server before the web page reaches your browser. All the computational requirements are met by the server, and a neat, tidy product is then delivered to your computer.

So far we have had a look at some of the front-end design principles that are used to develop user-friendly, functional and beautiful interfaces for us to use when we visit a website. However, for very complex websites, most of the code is written for the server and is executed on the *back-end*. This code is not concerned with how attractive the results are, since no user ever has to see them. Rather, this code is there to handle server-side functionality, such as interacting with a database, storing files, processing user data, handling email, processing payments, collecting data from external websites, providing user authentication and much more.

For these tasks, we need a new language. Languages used server-side are known as 'server-side scripting languages' and the most popular is PHP. Others exist, such as Perl, and Ruby, as well as Python, which we are already well acquainted with.

In addition to scripting language, server-side programs for websites typically use a database 'querying language'. These are very high-level languages used to create, read, update and delete data from databases and tables that are stored on a server, and we'll be introduced to one a bit later on.

PHP

A web server, as we have already seen, is a server which responds to HTTP requests from a client within a network. Web server software is required to be installed on a web server. This is software which binds to a HTTP port on your server, listens for HTTP requests and knows how to answer them.

PHP is the most popular scripting language on the web and it is a language which sits on top of your web server software. When a client requests a page that contains PHP code, your web server executes it and sends the resultant web page (without PHP) to your client using a POST request.

Like Python, PHP is a scripting language, which means that it's not compiled before it is executed, but rather is processed and executed on-the-fly. It is a fairly cryptic language in terms of its syntax so we would not spend too long getting confused about it, but we'll learn enough to give us a general idea of how it can be used to:

- Take information from web-based forms,
- Authenticate and track users,
- Handle commends and threaded discussions on a website,
- Serve different pages to people on different devices.

As I have said before, this book is not intended to be a set-by-step tutorial, but if you want to execute this code yourself you will need a web server installed on your computer and you'll also need to install PHP. If you're on a Windows machine, you can install a WampServer (www.wampserver.com/en), or if you're on a Mac you can use MAMP (www.mamp.info). If you get stuck, there are plenty of tutorials out there to help you get a working web server and PHP environment set up on your own machine.

One of the wonderful things about PHP is that it lets you embed your code within a HTML page, to be executed when the page is requested. PHP code is enclosed within the tags shown in the basic example below. '<?php' is used to open a block of PHP code, and '?>' closes it.

```
<html>
 <body>
       <?php
       echo "Hello, world!";
       ?>
 </body>
</html>
```

This basic example simply prints the text "Hello, world!" to the screen when the page is requested.

As we saw when we were learning Python, variables are the bread and butter of a program, as they are used to store the very data that a program is written to process. PHP supports a number of different variable types, including integers (INTs), strings, floating point numbers, and arrays, and, similar to Python, is able to automatically figure out the type of variable being used. PHP variables must always be preceded with a dollar sign ($) and begin with either a letter or an underscore followed by any sequence of letters or numbers.

Here's an example to illustrate a few new things, including PHP variables. Our HTML page contains a <body> element which holds both a paragraph element with an extract from a transcript of a play and a block of PHP code.

```
<html>
<body>
      <p>Sergeant: Good afternoon, remind me of your name
soldier.</p>

      <?php
      // Define some variables
      $name = ‘James’;
      $rank = ‘officer’;
      $serialNumber = 56783;
      // Print an output
      echo “<p>Officer: I am <b>$name</b>, an <i>$rank</i>.
My serial number is: <b>$serialNumber</b>.</p>”;
      ?>

</body>
</html>
```

First, within the PHP code, we make a helpful comment to explain what the next few lines do. This is done using the double backslash in PHP (‘//’). We then define the variables ‘$name’, ‘$rank’ and ‘$serialNumber’. In this example, ‘$serialNumber’ is initialised with a number, whereas the first two variables are initialised with strings. PHP understands this and automatically creates two string variables and one INT variable.

Next, the example above uses the ‘echo’ keyword to print some text to the screen. In essence, the ‘echo’ keyword replaces the PHP block which encloses it with the string that then follows. In our case, the string is enclosed within a paragraph element, denoted by the ‘<p></p>’ tags at either end. Within these tags are included two bold elements ‘<b>’ which print bold text to the screen, and an italics element ‘<i>’ which prints text in italics to the screen. Within these elements are the variables that we’ve previously defined. PHP automatically converts these variables to the correct format for printing as a string, so the inclusion of these variables within our string enables the contents of the variables to be displayed as part of the total string that's being printed by the 'echo' keyword.

As a brief exercise say out loud (or write on a piece of paper) the output of this program and try to visualise what you would see.

As we've seen in Chapter 9, there are two ways that a browser can send information to a web server.

- A GET request
- A POST request

Both the GET and POST requests are used to request data from the web server. When you use your browser to navigate to www.google.com, this address forms the basis of a page request.

The GET Method

You may have noticed that sometimes when browsing the Internet, the URL in the address bar of your browser contains a series of key/value pairs after a '?' symbol. An example is the URL below which forms the basis of a GET request to Google.

```
https://www.google.com/search?q=facebook
```

As you can see, we're using the HTTPS (encrypted HTTP) protocol to access Google's search page, but from here things may get unfamiliar. This base URL is appended with '?q=facebook'. Here the '?' denotes the end of the page URL and the beginning of a list of key/value pairs. In our case, the key 'q' is set to 'facebook'.

Pages written in PHP on the server may contain variables that can be assigned by the client upon the requesting of the page. We have taken a brief look at PHP variables above, but they have all been assigned by us inside the PHP code of the page. These key/value pairs allow us to set the value of some parameters in the PHP code when we access the page from the web server.

In the example above, there is a variable 'q' inside the PHP code of the Google search page, which is open to be set by the user. We've set this variable equal to the string 'facebook'. Google then takes this string and uses it as the search phrase before returning a list of search results.

Try putting this URL into your browser and observing the results. You can even change the value of this parameter and watch Google return a different set of search results.

When a user requests a page using their own information, a GET request encodes this information into the URL of the page request. So, when I type 'Facebook' into the search box on Google's home-page, my browser encodes this string into the URL of the page request producing a request similar to the example above.

You may well be wondering how exactly this all looks in PHP. If my PHP variables can be set by the user requesting the page, how exactly do we choose what to do with those variables? The example below serves to illustrate exactly what it means to produce a GET request and handle it in PHP on the server.

This example is a complete PHP page — it displays a form to the user, allows them to enter data, this is submitted to the server and then sent back to the client as HTML.

```
<?php
 if( $_GET["name"] || $_GET["age"] )
 {
  echo "Welcome". $_GET['name']. "<br />";
  echo "You are". $_GET['age']. " years old.";
  exit();
 }
?>
<html>
<body>
 <form action="<?php $_PHP_SELF ?>" method="GET">
 Name: <input type="text" name="name" />
 Age: <input type="text" name="age" />
 <input type="submit" />
 </form>
</body>
</html>
```

Let's look at the HTML part first. We've defined a '<form>' element which displays data entry widgets which allow the user to enter data. The 'action' attribute in this example has been set to whatever is resolved by the PHP code `<?php $_PHP_SELF ?>`. The variable used here is an internal PHP variable which is always equal to the name of the page that it's called from. This 'action' attribute thus defines the page that our form submits to. The use of this internal variable will ensure that the form always submits to this page, even if its name changes. We've set the 'method' attribute to 'GET' which denotes that we wish to use a GET request as opposed to a POST request when submitting our form.

The <form> element contains two '<input>' elements. These are input boxes for text input (denoted by the value of the 'type' attribute). We've defined their names to be 'name' and 'age' which depict the meaning of the data they're to contain. In the closing tag of the form, we've specified the 'type' to be 'submit' which automatically places a 'Submit' button at the bottom of the form to execute the GET request.

```
<html>
<body>
 <form action="<?php $_PHP_SELF ?>" method="GET">
 Name: <input type="text" name="name" />
 Age: <input type="text" name="age" />
 <input type="submit" />
 </form>
</body>
</html>
```

Turning our attention to the PHP code above, we notice first of all the keyword 'if'. This keyword performs the same logical operation for decision making as the Python equivalent. In PHP, an 'if' statement must be enclosed in brackets. The two parallel bars (||) are PHP's logical 'OR' symbol, which ensures the condition resolves to be true if either of the conditions on each side of it are true.

```
<?php
 if( $_GET["name"] || $_GET["age"] )
 {
  echo "Welcome". $_GET['name']. "<br />";
  echo "You are". $_GET['age']. " years old.";
  exit();
 }
?>
```

Each side of this symbol are two variables which access elements in the internal PHP dictionary '$_GET'. This is a variable which is initialised when the page receives a GET request. Every key/value pair in the URL of the page request is added as a key/value pair to the '$_GET' variable which then allows us to access those values from within our PHP code. For example, when we use the phrase '$_GET("name")' in PHP, we're looking for the value in the $_GET dictionary variable with the key 'name'. Since our form used a GET request, this value should be the contents of the 'name' input field on the HTML page when the form was submitted.

In other words, what we're saying in this example of PHP is "if the value of the element in the '$_GET' dictionary with key 'name' is set (evaluates to true), or if the value of the element in the '$_GET' dictionary with key 'age' is set, execute the chunk of code between the curly brackets".

Within this block, we print 'Welcome', followed by the value of the 'name' parameter in the GET request, followed by a <br> element. We then print 'You are', followed by their submitted age, followed by the string ' years old.'.

Try writing our on a piece of paper the full string that would be printed if you entered your name and age.

Three things to note:

- The <br> element is a break, which simply inserts a new line
- Lines of PHP code which execute something, must end with a semi-colon ';'
- Exit() is a built-in PHP function which stops the execution of the script

- The dot operator (.) is the symbol that PHP uses to concatenate strings

The POST Method

Unlike the GET request, the POST request does not send the user's data in the URL of the page request, instead it sends it to the header of the HTTP request. This means that any data the user wants to send to the PHP page on the web server is stored within the HTTP request. You do not need to worry about what a HTTP request is exactly at this stage, but just remember that data sent using a POST request is not sent in the page request.

Data sent using a POST request is not limited in its size, as it is in a GET request, so when large files need to be uploaded from a client to a web server through a website, a POST request should be used.

The example below is almost exactly the same to our previous example of a GET request, but the word GET is replaced with POST.

```
<?php
 if( $_POST["name"] || $_POST["age"] )
 {
  echo "Welcome". $_POST['name']. "<br />";
  echo "You are". $_POST['age']. "years old.";
  exit();
 }
?>
<html>
<body>
 <form action="<?php $_PHP_SELF ?>" method="POST">
 Name: <input type="text" name="name" />
 Age: <input type="text" name="age" />
 <input type="submit" />
 </form>
</body>
</html>
```

The form submission in HTML and the accessing of the key/value pairs in the POST request are exactly the same as before. The only difference is in the way that this data is sent. As noted, data sent in a POST request is not in the URL, but in the HTTP request. This leads to a much cleaner URL. POST requests are also typically better for sending sensitive data such as passwords and personal information, since this data will not be visible in the URL of the page.

PHP is a hugely powerful and flexible language for the web. It is the most popular server-side scripting language for websites and offers a range of features for almost anything you'll need to do in terms of handling data.

SQL

Data is the primary asset that the Internet handles. Arguably is it the only asset that it can handle. The Internet is jam-packed with data and everyone with a PC and a network cable can access it. All of this information needs to be stored somewhere and in a format which makes it easy and fast to access.

Structured Query Language (SQL) is a high-level languages designed for quickly creating, reading, updating and deleting large sets of data, stored in relational databases. It is used by server-side applications, so a brief introduction to it at this point will complement our basic understanding of PHP.

The concept to understand is this — a query in SQL is defined and executed in PHP, using an SQL database which either creates, reads, updates or deletes data stored in that database. If the SQL query reads data, for instance, the data is returned when the SQL is executed in PHP, so that data held in a database can be processed in PHP and later sent to a user over the Internet. You should be aware that SQL can be used in a range of different programming languages, but since we're learning PHP we will see some examples of its use in that context.

In order to become acquainted with SQL using PHP, we'll first get to grips with the syntax of SQL, and then see how we can run SQL queries in PHP.

Often in a 'relational database', data is best stored in collections of tables. Hence, a relational database contains database objects called 'tables' which contain data related to each other in some way. These tables contain columns and rows — items of data are stored in rows, and are related by similarities in each column.

Databases often contain more than one table. For example, a company selling sports clothing online might use a database to store all the information relating to their customers and to the products they have for sale. They may have a table called 'Customers' to store all the information they have about their customers, and a table called 'Products' to store all the information about their products.

The table 'Products' might look like the following, which contains four columns and five different records:

ID	Type	Brand	Stock
1	T-shirt	Nike	23
2	Jumper	Umbro	81
3	Shorts	Nike	6
4	T-shirt	Adidas	2
5	Trainers	Karrimor	29

The following SQL query selects all of the records in this table called 'Products'.

```
SELECT * FROM Products;
```

It's worth noting that SQL statements are not case sensitive, so we could just as easily use the statement below to achieve the same:

```
select * from Products;
```

When this statement is executed the following data will be returned — the entire contents of the 'Products' table:

ID	Type	Brand	Stock
1	T-shirt	Nike	23
2	Jumper	Umbro	81
3	Shorts	Nike	6
4	T-shirt	Adidas	2
5	Trainers	Karrimor	29

To return only a selection of the columns, for instance 'Stock', we can use the following:

```
SELECT Type, Stock FROM Products;
```

This will return the following:

Type	Stock
T-shirt	23
Jumper	81
Shorts	6
T-shirt	2
Trainers	29

Both of the commands we've used here return every row of the data, even if — as in the example above — we only want a subset of the columns available. To find particular rows, we can use the WHERE clause, which will select data where a certain column has a particular value. In our clothing store, for instance, the owners may wish to see a list of the stock they have with the 'Nike' brand. They would use the WHERE clause to add a requirement that the 'Brand' column of the record be equal to 'Nike'.

```
SELECT * FROM Products WHERE Brand='Nike';
```

Which will return the following:

ID	Type	Brand	Stock
1	T-shirt	Nike	23
3	Shorts	Nike	6

If the clothing store then orders in ten items of a new product, six hats from Puma for instance, they will need to insert a new record to the database. This can be done by using the 'INSERT' clause as follows:

```
INSERT INTO Products VALUES (6, 'Hat', 'Puma', 10);
```

When the user selects the entire table again the new item will appear in its place.

```
SELECT * FROM Products;
```

ID	Type	Brand	Stock
1	T-shirt	Nike	23
2	Jumper	Umbro	81
3	Shorts	Nike	6
4	T-shirt	Adidas	2
5	Trainers	Karrimor	29
6	Hat	Puma	10

As new stock comes in, the 'Stock' column of a particular item may need to be updated. Let's say the store has just received 100 more Adidas T-shirts bringing the total in stock to 102. In this case, another clause can be used and yes, you've guessed it! It's an UPDATE clause.

```
UPDATE Products SET Stock=102 WHERE Brand='Adidas' AND
  Type='T-shirt';
```

This statement updates the table 'Products' by setting the 'Stock' column to the value 102 for all records where the 'Brand' column is 'Adidas' and the 'Type' column is 'T-shirt'. The table below illustrates the effect of this UPDATE.

To remove a record from the database entirely, the owner of the sportswear store can use the DELETE clause.

ID	Type	Brand	Stock
1	T-shirt	Nike	23
2	Jumper	Umbro	81
3	Shorts	Nike	6
4	T-shirt	Adidas	102
5	Trainers	Karrimor	29
6	Hat	Puma	10

```
DELETE FROM Products WHERE Type='T-shirt';
```

Here we are telling our SQL database to delete all records from the 'Products' table where the 'Type' column is equal to 'T-shirt'. Since two of the products are T-shirts, this statement deletes both of these records from the table. By selecting the remaining records in the database we can see that they're been removed.

ID	Type	Brand	Stock
2	Jumper	Umbro	81
3	Shorts	Nike	6
5	Trainers	Karrimor	29
6	Hat	Puma	10

We now have a basic understanding of how to manipulate data in a relational database, but how did we get this database there in the first place? And how did we choose what data the table contained? It's well worth noting how to create a database and how to add our own tables to it.

To create a database, we use the CREATE DATABASE statement:

```
CREATE DATABASE CustomerDatabase;
```

In the example above, we've simply created a database with the name CustomerDatabase, but we can call it whatever we want. If our 'Products' table was in a database called 'Inventory', we could use a SHOW DATABASES statement to display a list of all our databases which would give us the following:

Database
information_schema
Inventory
CustomerDatabase
mysql

There are two surprising databases in here that you won't have been expecting. 'information_schema' and 'mysql' are both databases which hold information about our databases, specifically the particular SQL relational database that we're using, and the privileges of the users who can use the databases and tables. In general you can forget they exist.

Use the keyword USE to tell the database that you want to use a particular database.

From here, we're able to create a table within the 'CustomerDatabase' database using the CREATE TABLE statement.

```
CREATE TABLE Customers

(
   ID INT,
   LastName VARCHAR(255),
   FirstName VARCHAR(255),
   Address VARCHAR(255),
   Email VARCHAR(255)
);
```

The statement above could all be on one line, but is separated for clarity. The general format for the creation of a table is clear from this example. We define the name of the table after the CREATE TABLE statement, in this case 'Customers', and specify the column names and data types of each column inside the brackets that follow. The name of the column is defined first, followed by the type of data being stored. Each column is separated by a comma. A number of additional commands can be used in the definition of each column which add specific requirements to the format of the data. In the example used above, the ID is an INT and the other columns are of type VARCHAR(255). An integer in SQL can be considered the same as a Python integer — a whole number. A VARCHAR is a VARiable CHARacter field and the number 255 denotes that its length cannot exceed 255 characters. It is essentially a Python string.

SQL in PHP

So far, our only use of SQL has been by manually typing in the SQL statements to retrieve our required data. In order to automate this process, we can specify the SQL statements in PHP and have them executed automatically in code.

The following example shows a block of PHP code which connects to an SQL database, prepares a query to execute, executes it and finally sets a variable equal to the data returned by the database.

```
<?php
$con = mysql_connect("localhost", "username", "password");
$sql = "SELECT * FROM Products";
$result = mysql_query($sql, $con);
// Do something with $result containing contents of
  Products table
mysql_close($con);
?>
```

To explain — in PHP, the most common relational database is MySQL, a database which uses the SQL language to query it. We can use the function 'mysql_connect' in PHP to connect to the database. In this case, we're assuming we have our database on our local computer 'localhost', and are connecting with the username 'username' and password 'password'. Clearly there are some security problems with these credentials, but for the purposes of getting us familiar with SQL in PHP, let's stick with it. The connection object is returned from this function and is labelled $con for connection.

The variable $sql is a string which is initialised with the string 'SELECT * FROM Products', which is our query. The MySQL function 'mysql_query' is then used to execute our query using the established connection, and the variable $result is given the result in the form of a PHP 'resource' object. Finally the connection is closed and the PHP script terminates.

This same procedure can be used to connect to any database, access any table and to automatically change it in any way as required. Let us see an example of how we can print the contents of the 'Products' table to a HTML page.

```
<html>
<head>
</head>
<body>
<?php
$con = mysql_connect("localhost", "username", "password");
$sql = "SELECT * FROM Products";
$result = mysql_query($sql, $con);
while ($row = mysql_fetch_assoc($result)) {
  echo 'ID:'.$row['ID'].'<br>';
  echo 'Type:'.$row['Type'].'<br>';
  echo 'Brand:'.$row['Brand'].'<br>';
  echo 'Stock:'.$row['Stock'].'<br>';
  echo '<br>'
}
mysql_close($con);
?>
<body>
<html>
```

In the example above, we've inserted a PHP 'while' loop into our original example. The MySQL function 'mysql_fetch_assoc' accepts a 'resource' object — in our case '$result' — and returns an associative array (similar to a Python 'Dictionary' object). This is the next line of the SQL table, where each element of the array is a record's column in the table. This function returns 'false' as soon as there are no more rows to return. In the 'while' loop for each row, we print a string describing the data type and the value of the corresponding column in the database, which is accessed by the name of the column as a key.

When this code is executed, the result is a list of the entire contents of the 'Products' table, displayed to the user's HTML page.

Hopefully, the ways that PHP can be used as a scripting language to handle a user's interaction with a server-side database through web applications are becoming clear to you. There are countless possibilities of how this can be used in the real world to create powerful web platforms including social media websites, online work collaboration services, content distribution services, media entertainment websites and many more.

This part of your introduction to programming has been an extremely brief first-contact with networks, sockets, HTML, CSS, JavaScript, PHP and SQL, and you'll by no means be proficient in these languages after this limited exposure; however you should now have some understanding of the basic uses of each of these languages, as well as how each of them is used in the development of a web-based software product.

Questions

1. Where is PHP code executed, on the server or client device?
2. What is the difference between a GET request and a POST request?
3. What SQL query can I use to select the entire contents of an SQL database?
4. How can you execute SQL statements from within PHP code? Consider the HTML tags and PHP functions used.

What's Out There?

Chapter 10

Amazing Algorithms

Algorithms — sets of instructions that float between mathematical equations and computer programs — have saturated our lives in almost every area, even if we are not aware of it. Whether encrypting our credit card details to send securely over the Internet, or taking us to a foreign destination as part of our satellite navigation system, the vast majority of present day technology would not work without these highly sophisticated processes.

When you hear the word 'algorithm', there are a number of responses you might have. You might immediately understand what we're talking about because you studied computer science at university. Or you may know that companies like Google and Microsoft use them to do clever things, but you are not really sure what they are. Or you may be tempted to run away in terror, because those four syllables are alien and hostile to your ears. If you fall in either of the last two categories, this chapter is for you.

An algorithm is a conceptual set of steps, designed to solve a problem or reach a goal in an efficient manner. In the context of computer science they are typically relatively small pieces of code, which use data in some special way to produce a meaningful output.

It's important to understand the idea behind designing an algorithm and understand how some specific algorithms work. Most programmers aren't developing algorithms as sophisticated as those used in a credit card data encryption or for a Google search, but they will need to deal with algorithms of their own on a daily basis. In our case, when creating 'for' loops and functions, we're writing our own algorithms, and we need to understand a few that are already out there to help us to write powerful and effective algorithms of our own.

PageRank

The broad idea of how Google's search algorithm works has been public knowledge for many years, despite the specific details of how it organises its search results remaining a closely guarded secret.

The algorithm Google uses is PageRank. Before Google, search engines used inefficient and ineffective algorithms to seek websites. Google's creation of the PageRank algorithm revolutionised the search engine and Google's popularity grew massively.

PageRank works by looking at all of the links on the Internet which point to a certain page, and counting how many of these links there are. A link to a page can be considered a vote for that page's quality or a recommendation to visit it. This means that the more links a page has pointing to it, the greater its PageRank will be.

This is ingenious, but it is not the end of the story. PageRank adds another dimension which has to do with the value of a vote. If a stranger at the pub recommends a particular restaurant, it may carry some weight and I may well go and check it out, however if a world-renowned chef recommends a restaurant, his authority means that the recommendation will have a far greater value. This is similar to PageRank's second feature. Pages with a high PageRank confer a higher PageRank themselves. If a friend's blog points to my blog, it won't count for much in terms of my overall PageRank. But if the highly ranked website like the BBC or Oxford University do, that has a far greater value, and therefore my own PageRank is boosted.

Take a look at the illustration on next page. Each page in the diagram represents a web page. The numbers on the page represent the PageRank of that particular page — i.e. the weight that that particular website has when 'voting' for another page. The arrows between pages represent links to other pages, and the numbers by the arrows are the weight that a particular link has when linking to another page.

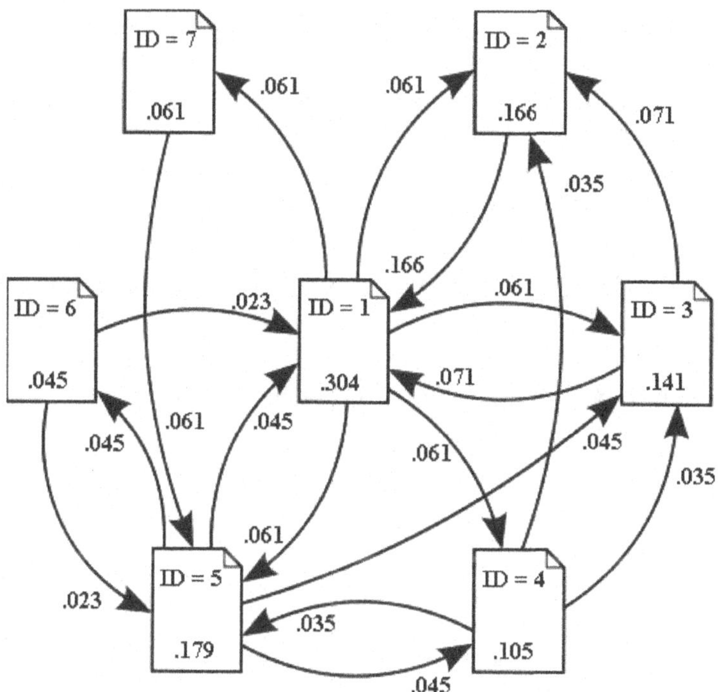

Let us take the page with ID = 1 as an example. There are 4 links which point to this page, and their combined weight gives the PageRank of 0.304. Since there are five links on this page which point to external pages, the PageRank is divided between these five pages, contributing an average of 0.061 to the PageRank of each of the pages it has links to. This is the basic concept behind Google's success with search.

There are numerous additional complexities that Google has added to its search algorithm, but Google's initial search feature remains its most important.

Sorting

One of the most common operations needing to be performed on data by programmers is sorting. The most intuitive way to order a list of items it to find the smallest item and put it first, then find the second smallest and put it next, and so on. This algorithm is relatively slow, however, as the number of items (N) in the list increases the time taken to sort the list by a factor proportional to the number of items squared.

Fortunately, there are a great number of different sorting algorithms available that work more quickly. One such alternative is *merge sort*, which uses a 'divide and conquer' approach to sorting. Merge sort divides a list with length N into N sub-lists and repeatedly merges the sub-lists, comparing the first elements of each sub-list to be merged and then placing them in the correct position until all of the sub-lists have been merged into a single list.

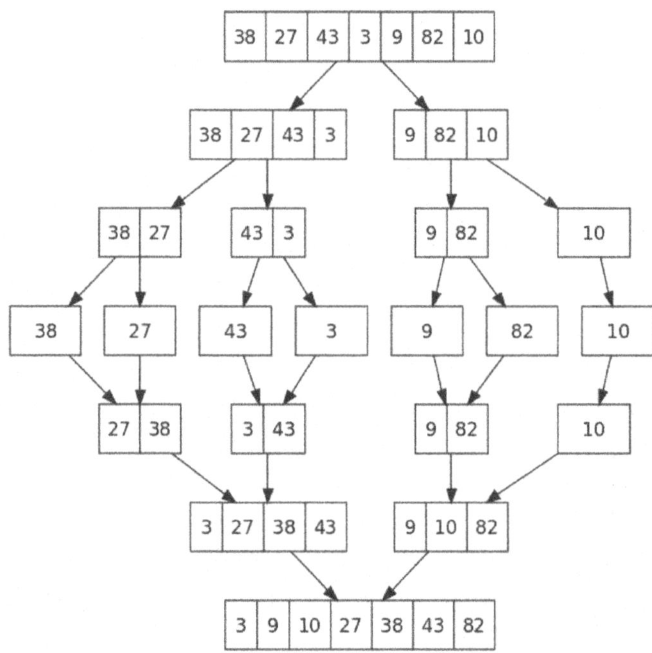

From the illustration above, we can see how merge sort works. The initial list is repeatedly split into sub-lists until there are N sub-lists. Then consecutive pairs of sub-lists are merged in their sorted order until the list is fully reconstructed.

Shortest Path

Algorithms for finding the shortest path from one point to another have been studied for years and there are many available. These algorithms are used everywhere, from finding the best running route, to identifying the quickest way to get home from work, to recommending the nearest place to find a fast food restaurant on a Friday night.

Consider a summer Sunday afternoon where you are planning a running route to the next village. You're unlikely to evaluate every possible route, since the universe would have suffered its heat death by the time you finished. In order to find the fastest route, quickly and effectively, a more intelligent algorithm is required.

One of the fastest algorithms for solving this path finding problem is known as 'Dijkstra's algorithm', named after the computer scientist Edsger Dijkstra. It is a fairly complex algorithm which involves the use of some unfamiliar data structures. It's based on the idea that every path segment has a 'cost' associated with travelling along it. This cost is usually related to the segments' length, but it can also be related to the 'terrain' or the 'traffic'. The shortest path is found by choosing the paths which have the least 'cost', and provide the greatest movement in the direction of the destination point. Using this algorithm to analyse a city of around 15,000 segments of road and 8,000 intersections, it takes about one second to compute a shortest path between two points.

Consider the map below. Try to use the idea of minimizing the cost (the numbers between the points) get from point five to point one.

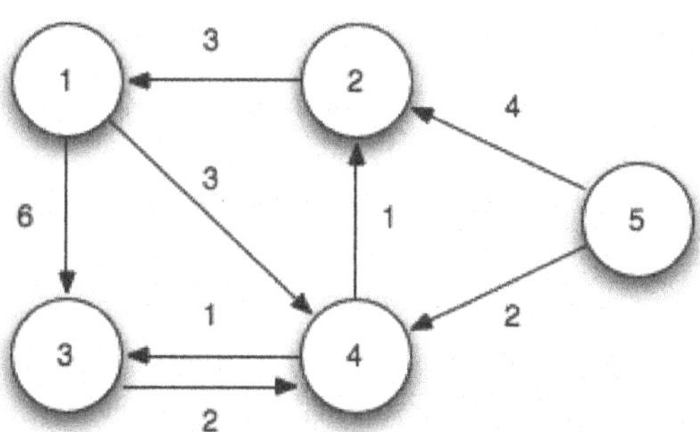

For many applications, even this algorithm is too slow, so more efficient and more complex algorithms are introduced. Typically in the design of these kinds of algorithms, a trade-off can be made between speed and accuracy. If an optimal route must be found at any cost, a less efficient but more accurate algorithm is required. However if the problem at hand can be solved by finding a path that is, say, 10% longer than the shortest path, then a much faster but possibly less accurate algorithm can be used.

Artificial Intelligence

Some of the most powerful and advanced algorithms are seen in the field of artificial intelligence or AI. AI has become a bit of a buzzword in technology and calls to mind films like iRobot, depicting human-like robots taking over the world. If an iRobot is ever manufactured, it will surely depend upon a huge amount of AI, but robotics is by no means the only application of this kind of intelligent algorithm.

Put simply, artificial intelligence is the capacity of a computer to exhibit the computational behaviour of humans. In the field of AI, the computer which exhibits this 'intelligence' is known as an intelligent *agent*. This agent typically perceives something relating to its environment and, based on this, makes decisions which enhance its performance.

This environment may not be a physical environment, but rather a context in which it is designed to operate, such as on a server to process user-data or in a handheld mobile device to understand a user's voice commands.

The field of AI is particularly young and immature. There are a host of applications of AI in engineering, medicine, education, transport and communication that could revolutionise these sectors. While it is already having a substantial influence, so much more can be done.

The central problems for AI researchers is to find ways for computers to perform very 'human-like' actions, such as reasoning, planning, understanding, learning and perception. Trivial for the human mind, these are incredibly difficult for computers to perform.

At present, no computer can fully exhibit full artificial intelligence (so as to completely simulate human behaviour). In some fields, such as assembly plants, computers can hugely outperform humans in terms of speed and accuracy, but, so far, they are only capable of performing very limited tasks.

As we have seen, algorithms are fundamental in solving many complex problems. We've only touched on a small subset of popular algorithms that you may end up using at some point. Many are unique to a specific problem and you'll need to learn to be able to break up problems into the steps required to solve them. However, many algorithms are available for common problems — they have already been solved for you. All you need to do is find where it's been done, and then borrow the code.

Questions

1. What is an algorithm and what are they used for?
2. What information does the PageRank algorithm use to rank a website?
3. How does the merge sort algorithm use a 'divide and conquer' approach to sort items on a list?
4. What modern applications does a shortest path algorithm have? How can it be used to solve real world problems?
5. How does Dijkstra's shortest path algorithm chose which path to take when it approaches a junction?
6. How could some form of artificial intelligence be used to solve a problem you face on a daily basis?

Chapter 11

Programming Languages, Libraries and Frameworks

A few years ago, I set myself the challenge of learning French using an audio resource I found online. Needless to say, I failed in achieving my goals; however I did learn that I already know a lot of French just by knowing English. A lot of English words share a common origin with French words, leading to many similarities. For example, many English words that end in -ly such as 'absolutely' or 'intensely' have equivalents in French ending with -ment. '*Absolument*' is the French word for 'absolutely' and '*intensément*' is the French word for 'intensely'.

Programming languages such as Python can be compared in somewhat comparable ways. They have sets of understood vocabulary and syntax structures, and if the rules of the language are not correctly followed, the language cannot be understood.

We have already looked at a broad set of programming languages, including JavaScript, PHP and HTML, so it would not surprise you to hear that just as there are many human languages, there are also many programming languages. Each language was designed for a particular reason and each, therefore, has a particular purpose. Some programming languages are better than others for different tasks, and some are capable of things that others simply do not have the vocabulary to do.

This chapter introduces a few new languages. We will not be learning them here, but rather finding out what they can do, and what situations they are best for. By knowing the names of a few popular languages and by understanding both their capabilities and limitations, you will be far more equipped to find which is the right language to learn for the particular programming challenges you face.

Modern development projects can usually be categorised into one of the following categories: 'web', 'mobile' or 'desktop' applications. Web applications are software products delivered across the Internet and viewed in a web browser, including social media websites, online news applications and online forums. Mobile applications are delivered to mobile devices, such as phones and tablets, and are designed specifically for the smaller screen-size and hardware capabilities of such devices. Desktop applications can be thought of as traditional software running on a desktop PC or laptop, and exploiting the high computational power and larger display size of these devices. So, what is the best programming language to get your development project up and running?

Web Ideas

With mobile devices are becoming more widespread and applications for our smartphones are being released all the time, new web based tools and start-ups are gaining in popularity. In general, a piece of software can be developed more quickly as a web app than a traditional desktop application and is also more accessible, so much of these new applications are provided as web services hosted on a server.

We have already looked at PHP as a server-side scripting language. Now we are going to look at using Python on the server-side. We're also going to look at a language called Ruby. With these languages you can create anything from hotel booking websites, to niche blogging applications, to new online marketplaces.

Bootstrap

When we looked at HTML and CSS we were introduced to the <div> tag which we could style using CSS. Bootstrap is a free CSS framework developed by Twitter which helps developers to design beautiful web pages quickly. t's incredibly easy to use. It requires no prior designing knowledge and assumes that all you are trying to do is write some flexible and attractive HTML.

In essence, it is a pre-written CSS style sheet with support for some popular JavaScript tools. All you need to do is place the required HTML mark-up as attributes in the correct element tags and you're good to go. There are some fantastic tutorials for Bootstrap available online and if you end up needing a beautiful user interface for your web application, Bootstrap is the way to go.

JavaScript and jQuery

jQuery is a powerful JavaScript library which improves and simplifies a range of common JavaScript activities. It provides simple methods for attaching event handlers to elements of a page — such as buttons or <div> tags — to allow them to become interactive. jQuery also makes it easy to give your page simple animations. It provides methods for moving HTML elements when an event occurs, making them fade away, slide around, change colour or change content.

jQuery also provides easy use of a feature known in JavaScript known as 'Ajax' (Asynchronous JavaScript and XML). This is a very useful feature which allows content to be loaded from a server and sent to update the contents of a page, after the page has already loaded. It allows for the contents of a page to be updated with live data, without reloading the entire page. jQuery allows this feature of JavaScript to be used easily and robustly, using its own Ajax method. The Ajax feature of jQuery can also be used to make GET and POST requests, providing reliable, full-featured, and fully interactive communication with a server after a web page has already been loaded.

For providing user interaction, simple animations, Ajax and more, jQuery has a lot to offer. It can be easily picked up and will save you time and energy, and will ultimately give you a better result when you put your ideas into code.

Python and Django

Many developers would recommend that Python be the first language learnt by a novice, which is why it is the language on which the first two parts of this book are based. Using online programming games, Python is now the language that many schools are beginning to teach their students.

Compared to many other languages, it is extremely easy to pick up and the basics can be learned in a few days. However, in order to be a really excellent developer you'll need to go far beyond this. Fortunately, Python's simple syntax makes it easy to develop large systems much faster than if they were being implemented in other languages.

But, in order to develop a web application, Python is not enough by itself. You'll need a 'web application framework' in order to produce a robust and interactive web application using Python. A web application framework is an abstraction in which software providing generic or common functionality is used to minimise the time needed to develop a new application. Frameworks allow developers to focus on specific parts of their application, instead of on 'repeat codes' that are used everywhere. It allows them to create application-specific software more easily. This alleviates overheads associated with common activities performed in web development, by allowing developers to write code that's understandable, manageable, secure and robust, more quickly and easily.

Django is the most popular web application framework for developing web applications in Python. It is free, and follows the Model-View-Controller (MVC) architecture. This is a development pattern which is intended to increase the simplicity of web application development. It does this by separating the ways in which information is stored, presented and accessed by the user into separate components. Data is stored as models, presented using views and accessed using controllers.

The diagram on next page illustrates the behaviour of the MVC architecture. A user's browser requests the web page on the server hosting the web application. The user then sees the 'view', which is the part of the web application that includes the HTML, CSS and JavaScript, which display the content clearly, interactively and aesthetically to the user. This is sent from the web server to the client's browser.

When a user interacts with the website in some way (such as by submitting a form), the GET or POST request sent by the user is

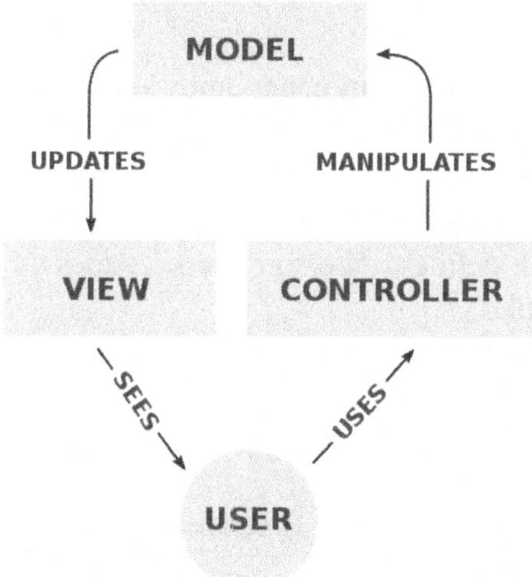

handled by a *controller* on the server. The controller understands the user's interaction with the website and knows how to handle it. On the server, the controller then accesses *models* which are also stored on the web server. These models represent the data that the user is interacting with and are usually linked to an SQL database or similar.

From here, the view is kept up-to-date by responding to the user's form submission and updating the web application's models. Each time the user requests a new page from the web application, the view is updated to display the most up-to-date models. Web application frameworks that follow the MVC architecture use this pattern to handle the web application's storage and handling of data. It makes the process of implementing and deploying a prototype web application much faster.

Pros

- Powerful language
- Fast scripting
- Widespread usage and support
- Easy to learn
- Many pre-written modules

Cons

- None

Ruby and Rails

Ruby is a programming language quite similar to Python. It is a scripting language and as such its own Ruby interpreter. Its syntax shares many similarities with Python, and the language is also very easy to learn. To illustrate Ruby, the example below shows a small Ruby script which defines a 'Person' class, creates a Person and prints its instance variables.

```
// Example Ruby program

class Person
  def initialize(firstName, lastName)
      @firstName = firstName
      @lastName = lastName
  end
end
person = Person.new("Joe","Bloggs")
print person
```

Ruby offers a fantastic MVC web application framework called 'Ruby on Rails'. Rails is similar to Django in its capabilities, structure and usage, and is extremely easy to use and understand. The documentation for Rails is excellent and you'll find many books and online tutorials that will take you through using the application. Facebook is an obvious example of a great web application using PHP, however there are many companies that are using the Django or Ruby on Rails frameworks for their time-saving and usability benefits.

Pros

- Easy to pick up
- Large community
- Wide ranging features and capabilities
- Powerful

Cons

- None

Mobile Ideas

If your idea is web based, we've just seen two of many fantastic frameworks for giving you the tools you need to create powerful web applications quickly. With Bootstrap it's easy to make your web app available on mobile devices, adjusting for their smaller screen sizes and for touch screens. But Bootstrap is not sufficient.. Many ideas require the graphics, computational power and sensors that are only available through newly developed mobile applications.

The two most popular mobile platforms are Apple's iOS and Google's Android. Microsoft has released a mobile operating system (OS) called Windows Phone 8, but so far it has not been well received. We'll cover the language used on Windows Phone 8 under 'Desktop Ideas'.

Traditionally, a start-up would need to develop separate applications for two or three of these mobile platforms, but now there are a lot of cross-platform languages, frameworks and converters that make life easier, by developing cross-platform applications quickly. The faster you can prototype a Minimum Viable Product (MVP), the faster your product will be able to be used. However, there are always restrictions or compromises that have to be made when using cross-platform frameworks and often they reduce the quality of whatever it is you're producing.

So, for many (if not most) mobile development projects, it still makes a lot of sense to develop applications separately on each platform. Let us look at some of the languages you can use.

Objective-C

Apple uses a language called Objective-C for most of the development done on its devices. The Apple iPhone is no exception, so to develop an iOS application it's best to learn Objective-C. It's a language that has gained a tremendous amount of popularity in the last few years. It is a general-purpose, object-oriented programming language, that adds many additional features to a language called C. Objective-C is primarily developed using the Mac OS X application Xcode which is available for free in the app store on a Mac. It can be used to create all kinds of iOS applications including social networks, marketplaces and high-performance 3D gaming applications.

The learning curve with Objective-C is a steep one and it is harder to learn than Python or Ruby, but it is one of the best languages to learn to get your mobile app idea up and running.

```
// Example Objective-C program

#import <Foundation/Foundation.h>

int main(void) {
        int x = 1;
        int y = 2;
        int sum = x + y;
        printf("The sum is %d", sum);
        NSLog(@"Hello, World! \n");
        return 0;
}
```

The code above demonstrates a small Objective-C application. This example imports the 'Foundation' library which contains the definition of the 'NSLog' function and prints the sum of two integers to the screen. The '@' symbol before the string inside the argument for 'NSLog' denotes the beginning of an 'NSString' which is a special string object. The last line of this example returns the integer 0 to the process that executed this program, denoting the successful completion of its execution.

The use of Objective-C for iOS application development can get rather involved and it may take time for a beginner to get to grips with using the language — however the integrated development environment (Xcode) provided by Apple is exceptional. The iOS platform is extremely reliable and Xcode provides a range of powerful built-in tools to aid development. If you're in it for the long haul, Xcode and Objective-C provide one of the most enjoyable development experiences out there.

Pros

- Great documentation
- Great community and support for developers
- Uses Apple's development libraries
- Powerful language features

Cons

- Steep learning curve
- Not available on Windows or Linux

Java and Eclipse

Java is the primary language used to develop mobile applications for the Android platform. It is a relatively old language, but is still very widely used in a number of areas of industry. It is generally considered a good programming language for beginners to learn, but has a steeper learning curve than Python or Ruby. We could have included Java in the previous section, since it is also a popular server-side language and has its own web application MVC framework, however it's more commonly thought of as a mobile or desktop programming language.

```
// Example Android application written in Java

package com.coreservlets.helloandroid;

import android.app.Activity;
import android.os.Bundle;
import android.widget.TextView;

public class HelloAndroid extends Activity {
  @Override
  public void onCreate(Bundle savedInstanceState) {
    super.onCreate(savedInstanceState);
    TextView tv = new TextView(this);
    tv.setText("Hello, Android");
```

```
    setContentView(tv);
    System.out.println("Print statements and runtime
errors are shown in LogCat window in DDMS");
 }
}
```

The example above illustrates a very basic Android application written in Java. It shows the syntax used for importing Android libraries, and how to define a Java class. This basic program simply creates a 'TextView' object which is like a text box. It sets its text using the 'setText' method of the 'TextView' object and displays it on the screen.

The software most commonly used to create Android applications is Eclipse which is a free development application with a range of powerful features. Eclipse is available on all platforms, including Windows, Mac and Linux. This has obvious benefits in terms of development flexibility, but it does mean that the development environment provided by Google for Android development is less stable and doesn't offer the high-end quality for developers that Xcode does.

The Android user base is growing rapidly, as is the iOS user base, so there are many great opportunities available on this platform. If you're looking to develop an app, but don't have access to an Apple MacBook for iOS development, then Android is a great alternative.

Pros

- Powerful language
- Rich libraries available
- Great community and support
- A language for everything
- Free to use
- Extremely popular

Cons

- Steep learning curve
- Difficult syntax
- Difficult to use for prototyping
- Time inefficient development

Desktop Ideas

Mobile and web applications are without a doubt the most exciting platforms for developing new tools and services in software. Due to the portability of mobile devices and the cross-platform nature of the web, these methods of delivering services have the most potential to shape our culture, our lifestyles and our methods of working. But there are still a number of massive benefits to developing desktop applications, such as performance benefits and the ability for them to be used when the user is offline.

Increasingly, web languages such as HTML, CSS and JavaScript are being used to develop desktop applications, such as Windows 8 apps. This presents an exciting opportunity for developers who are already familiar with these web technologies. Yet incredible innovation is still being made using the more traditional 'compiled' desktop programming languages.

C++

C++ (pronounced "C plus plus") is a general purpose compiled language with a proud and impressive history. It's based on the popular compiled language C, has been around since the mid-1980s and is still used to develop a wide range of applications for the desktop. Its primary uses now enterprise systems, performance critical systems and embedded software. It is a language that has many benefits and features for multiple applications.

The example below is a C++ program which prints 'Hello World!' to the command line.

```
// Example C++ command-line program

#include <iostream>
int main()
{
 std::cout << "Hello World!" << std::endl;
 return 0;
}
```

When executed, the 'main' function here is executed. The '<<' is the C++ operator included in 'iostream' for appending a string to the command line.

In general, C++ is no longer the best option for developing interactive desktop applications, but it's well worth looking at if you want to understand how much of the more traditional software we use every day is designed and written.

Pros	**Cons**
• General purpose	• Steep learning curve
• Similar to Java	

C#

Pronounced "C sharp", this is the language to beat for developing almost any application on Windows. It is a simple, modern, general-purpose programming language that is an evolution of the C/C++ programming languages.

C# is the language to use for Windows desktop applications, but also it can be used through Microsoft's web application framework ASP.NET to develop web applications. It is also the primary language that applications for Microsoft's Windows Phone 7/8 platforms use, so you can also develop mobile applications in this language.

Here's an example of a basic C# application which prints the text 'Hello, World!' to the screen. We define a class with the name 'HelloWorld' and a function called main() within it. When a C# application is executed, the main() function is executed. This function uses the 'System.Console' object's method 'WriteLine' to print text to the screen.

```
// Example C# command-line application

public class HelloWorld
{
  public static void main()
  {
  System.Console.WriteLine("Hello, World!");
  }
}
```

You may have noticed that the syntax here is very similar to Java and C++. This makes it easy to learn all three for different applications. If you become familiar with Java for Android development, you'll find it easy to pick up C#.

Pros

- Modern and easy
- General purpose
- Used mobile, web and desktop
- Similar to Java and C++

Cons

- Older-style syntax
- Medium learning curve

Questions

1. What is Bootstrap and how does it make web development easier?
2. What is jQuery and what are its benefits over standard JavaScript?
3. What is Ajax used for, and what programming language does it use?
4. What is Django? How would you best describe the benefits of using an MVC framework for web development?
5. Which programming languages can you use for writing iOS applications and Android applications?
6. How do the syntax and common usages of C# and C++ differ from each other? Which would you use for developing a Windows Phone application?

Chapter 12
Big Ideas

Keeping up to date with the rapidly developing technology industry is often difficult. New products and services, delivering ground breaking technology are introduced to the market all the time, so remaining ahead of the curve involves a constant struggle.

Much of this innovation is happening in terms of the delivery of new products. These products are hardware platforms that require new applications. While it is the problem of electronic engineers to worry about creating the next generation of hardware, and it's the experienced computer programmers who will be writing the operating systems (OSs) to run on them. Fortunately for us, this innovation is constantly presenting developers with new kinds of opportunities.

The intention of this chapter on 'Big Ideas' in technology is to present to you the most important trends in the technology market, so that you are better able to understand the opportunities available. It's likely that much of this will be new to you and you may well feel out of your depth in thinking about entering this competitive arena, but the truth is that you should feel exactly the opposite.

As the technology industry is constantly developing there are constant opportunities to jump on the bandwagon. The majority of the developers and engineers in this sector have little expertise in industries other than their own, and many more are not able to solve the problems that interest them, but are instead working on larger (and more boring) enterprise projects.

You as the reader are as prepared as any experienced developer (and often more so) to identify the most important things you do at work, home, school, or as part of a club, and to identify the most frustrating aspects about doing them. Then you can think of a way these frustrations can be alleviated for you and others through software based technologies.

No doubt with future editions of this book these trends will change, however the fact remains that all of these areas are seeing growth at the moment. So let us see where technology's taking us.

Cloud Computing

The power of the Internet is in the capacity for files stored on a computer, one side of the world to be accessed by a computer on completely the other side of the world in a fraction of a second. This has meant that files maintained by organisations from around the world are potentially available to everyone. Traditionally the Internet has been used to access files belonging to another through their website, while desktop computers or laptops have been used to store personal files belonging to an individual user.

The term 'cloud computing' is everywhere, but few people feel they understand exactly what it means. In its simplest terms, cloud computing refers to the storing and accessing of data and programs on the Internet, instead of on your computer's hard drive. You may be thinking that that definition is the same as the definition of the Internet. And you had be right. The 'cloud' is just a metaphor for the Internet.

When you store data or run programs from your hard drive, that's called *local* storage and computing. Your data and programs are physically close to you (on your hard drive), so accessing that data is quick and easy. This is not the cloud. To be considered 'cloud computing' a user must be accessing data or running programs over the Internet. This means that the programs and files that they are looking for are stored on a remote server, and accessed over the network. Cloud computing opens up a host of possibilities for users, by allowing multiple users to access the same data over the Internet.

For programmers, cloud computing is one of the most exciting developments of the technology industry, because it provides the infrastructure upon which software can be written to solve previously unsolvable problems. These include allowing for multi-user collaboration; remote storage of personal documents to enable access from any Internet enabled device in the world; live video conferencing; online word processing, spreadsheet and graphics software which alleviate the need to install software locally; and much more.

Platforms and tools for developers such as the Google Cloud Platform, Microsoft Azure, Dropbox API and Amazon Web Services give developers the opportunity to produce software solutions for problems faced by people all over the world, and can instantly get them into the hands of those that need them most.

Big Data

The amount of information being collected and stored is increasing exponentially. Although the computational power of computers is also getting bigger, computers are increasingly unable to store and process data locally. 'Big data' is a term used to describe sets of data which are so large and complex that it becomes difficult to process using personal computers.

A huge amount of data is now publicly available. Wikipedia has given us accurate and detailed knowledge of anything we can think of. Twitter produces millions of public Tweets per day which tell us all sorts of information about people and their opinions. Census data, weather data, stock data and much more are all available to the world for free.

Organisations are also able to collect data from their customers. This includes their customer's activity on their website, address, age, purchasing history and more. Data such as this is valuable to companies to improve the quality of customer service, to create targeted advertising, to manage email correspondence, and to plan for company growth and minimise expenses.

Big data is changing the way that we do life and do business, and it's changing the way we work together.

Its use by an organisation leads to a competitive advantage through high quality customer feedback and marketing campaigns, and better strategic decision making through having more data about which decision would produce the best outcome.

The opportunities here for developers are in the areas in which big data can positively impact ourselves or others around us. If you're a teacher, big data can be used to analyse the correlation between various teaching styles and student exam results. If you're a sociologist, you will be able to use big data to analyse if there is a correlation between a happy childhood and a successful career. If you're a scientist, you can use big data to measure the link between alcohol consumption and the likely development of certain diseases.

For entrepreneurs, big data is perhaps one of the most valuable ideas out there. Value is added to raw data when it is combined with other data and analysed. Companies and organisations are always looking for innovative insights into the meaning of data, and you could build the start-up that provides them with the right tool.

The most powerful tool for developers in this arena is Apache Hadoop. This is an open source framework for processing large amounts of data in multiple storage locations. It is a complex framework and will take some degree of learning before it can be used effectively, but for many applications it can provide the most powerful mechanism for accessing and processing the data you need, to solve the problems you have set out to conquer.

The Internet of Things

For most of us in the Western World, our lives and homes have become saturated with devices and appliances which seek to make our lives easier and more enjoyable. Kitchen and living room appliances such as dishwashers, ovens, televisions and central heating systems are all bought to reduce the time or difficulty associated with cleaning, cooking, accessing entertainment, heating our homes and more. This is testimony to the fantastic developments in technology and has freed up time for us to do more of the things we enjoy.

More and more of these devices are becoming Internet enabled. Our phones, laptops, tablets and televisions are now more often than not wired-up to the web, offering us services previously unavailable.

'The Internet of Things' is a term used to describe the network of devices and appliances that are already connected to the Internet, and those that will be. Already smart thermostats are allowing our central heating systems to be controlled from our phones. Locks for our homes and cars are getting smarter, and are increasingly accessible through our phones too. More and more devices are being redesigned with Internet access, in order to increase the utility, accessibility, ease of use and security of our physical assets.

It would not be long before our beds, lighting, curtains and windows will be controllable over the Internet, and this presents developers in all walks of life with another arena in which to exercise their imagination and creativity.

Security and Data Privacy

In many areas of life benefits go hand-in-hand with risks and this is no less true than in the progress of technology. Basic risk management tells us that risk is related to two factors, the probability of an undesirable event occurring and the extent of the damage that would ensue should that event occur. If an event is likely to happen, but its consequences are not relevant; there is a low risk. Similarly if there is a highly undesirable consequence of an event occurring, yet a negligible probability that it will happen, the risk is low. However as the probability and the consequence of a vulnerability being exploited creep up, risks are increased.

Cloud computing and web technologies are leading to the centralisation of more and more of our everyday data and services. It is often advantageous for an organisation to have its activities increasingly automated and centralised. This typically involves exposing capabilities to Internet users, some malicious. Whether they are secure or not, there is no question that the consequences of modern computer systems being attacked by hackers have increased massively in recent years, since the amount of control over data and physical infrastructure that computers have has increased so much.

In addition, new technology is created all the time. There is no question that as computer systems are tested for security, improvements are made to make the age old systems more secure. However new software, websites, services and Internet enabled devices are coming to market almost daily and most undergo insufficient security tests before being commercially released and trusted by customers.

This provides an ever growing attack surface for malicious hackers to use in order to gain access to critical systems and exploit unknown vulnerabilities. Computer security is already a multi-billion dollar industry and will only increase as technology improves. We should expect to see significant increases in high profile security vulnerabilities exposed and it's important now more than ever to ensure that the programs we develop are secure.

New Learning Styles

Much progress is being made in the delivery of education, and the availability of knowledge, through technology. Websites such as Udemy, Coursera, The Open University and iTunes U are helping to deliver high quality degree-level courses for free. They allow individuals to choose for themselves the subjects to learn and avenues of learning to follow, Usually, there is no fee to pay.

Wikipedia and other knowledge sharing websites have changed the way we access information. Books, web pages, video tutorials, quizzes, flash cards and memory games on almost every topic are all over the web, and for many of us they are increasing our skill set, our employment prospects and our understanding of the most important things in life, helping us to learn efficiently, think critically and work effectively.

In countries where education is limited and adequate teachers are few and far between, technology is increasing access to knowledge for cultures that desperately need it. A poor understanding of what constitutes a healthy diet, or a lack of understanding about a cure for a known medical condition, can be a matter of life and death. Basic delivery of education through new learning styles has the capacity to revolutionise healthcare, farming, economic growth and sustainability in countries without the educational heritage many take for granted.

New learning styles are appearing regularly due to advances in technology and this trend will certainly continue. No one knows what our schools, universities and libraries will look like in 50 years time, but each of us can play a part in solving the problems we see in education by developing new tools for learning.

3D Printing

One of the primary factors slowing the rate of progress in industry is the speed of the iteration cycle of prototyping new products — that is, manufacturing. Manufacturing is slow, expensive and limited in its design capabilities and the shapes it can produce. 3D printing is the new hot topic in this field. It's a way to produce rapid prototypes of components by printing layers of a fine polymer on top of each other. This technology is still in its early stages and commercial 3D printers are only recently becoming available at affordable prices. But this makes it a hugely exciting time for anyone involved in manufacturing, teaching or art, who can use this new technology.

We should expect 3D printers to become more and more widespread in their usage and soon be introduced into homes. This will enable users to manufacture their own products instead of ordering them, leading to a number of potential developments in software for designing 3D products, as well as virtual marketplaces for virtual 3D products.

Wearable Technology and No-Touch Interfaces

From the moment of the release of the first Apple iPhone in 2007, developers all around the world began to realise the opportunities that smartphone technology would present. A brand new platform with fantastic support for developers, and the new accessibility of excellent hardware and sound operating systems (OSs), has been a gold mine for entrepreneurs. Even now Apple, Google and Microsoft are improving the support and capabilities offered to developers opening up new doors to solving previously inaccessible problems.

Do you want to know what the next big hit in tech is? From the section header you've probably already guessed it, but if I could put money on the next platform to shake up the software development industry it would be wearable technology. You can't put money on it, not in the primary sense at least. But that's not to say you can't bet on it.

Android Wear, a new OS for Android smart watches, has already hit the public domain and developers are beginning to produce applications which exploit the inherent capabilities of wearable technology by making new apps.

'No-Touch' is the idea that smart devices, particularly wearable devices, are best suited to be operated without the use of touch. That's not to say they shouldn't have touch screens or an on/off switch, but the focus is on a device which responds to the human voice in an intuitive way. This makes a range of activities possible, such as getting work done in the car without taking your eyes off the road or your hands off the wheel. It makes it possible to set a timer for the oven while your hands are covered in flour and eggs or change the music track you're listening to while cycling home from work.

By combining the programming capabilities of developers with the frustrations you face each day, each and every one of us is empowered to use our imagination to dream up ways to reduce those frustrations and maximise utility.

Questions

1. What is cloud computing and how can it improve productivity in businesses?
2. What is the primary value of Big Data? What examples can you give about interesting data that can be extracted from it?
3. What are the primary security considerations that are involved with the Internet of Things?
4. Try to come up with three ways that computer technology can be used to aid learning in developing countries.

5. How will 3D printing technology improve our design and manufacturing industry? What possibilities are there for using 3D printing in the home?
6. What benefits does wearable technology have in terms of usability, safety and technical capabilities?

Chapter 13

Where to Go from Here

If you have made it to this part of the book, 'Congratulations'! We've come a long way in our journey of learning to program practically for life. Let us quickly glance back at what we have covered. We have

- Looked at understanding what programming is and how practical it can be,
- Understood the idea behind using variables to store data and operations to manipulate it,
- Developed an understanding for what an 'If' statement does and what 'for' and 'while' loops are used for,
- Learned about methods and objects and how they can be used to model real world objects,
- Made a Graphical User Interface using wxPython,
- Learned about networks and web development using HTML, CSS, JavaScript, PHP and SQL,
- Discovered the uses of each major programming language,
- Been introduced to some popular algorithms,
- And had an insight into the direction that technology is heading.

That is a lot of stuff to cover in less than 200 pages — for instance, there is a huge amount about the language of Python that we did not cover. Now that you have dipped your toes into the world of programming, it is my sincere hope that you have been inspired and motivated to take what you've already grasped on to the next stage.

If that is the case, you can do two things from here on. They are (1) learn, and (2) do, and they go hand-in-hand.

Learn

It was never the intention of this book to be a comprehensive guide to all things code. Neither was it intended to be a textbook on Python, but rather a very broad explanation of practical programming worked through from the ground up. Programming can be a very abstract discipline and much of what we have covered is simple for the experienced developer, but complex for the novice. This book has attempted to approach those learning challenges with clear descriptions, illustrations and examples, in order to minimise the pain of learning to code.

This means that there is a great deal more work to be done. The best place to start is to get more familiar with Python. As you've seen, it's a language fit for purpose and it is easy to learn. There are many resources, both online and on paper that are geared up to helping you get familiar with Python. Find a book with a comprehensive set of explanations about all of Python's features, and work through some examples yourself in order to get more familiar with the principles you have been introduced to already.

Do

One of the best ways to learn is to do, and this is particularly true for programming. As well as using examples in a textbook or online tutorial, start working on your own project. It does not have to be large or difficult, but if you can find a project of your own that you care about, you can make it yours and use it as a productive and enjoyable way to develop your programming skills.

Here is a few examples of projects to get you started:

1. Make an attractive and informative website for your organisation, family business, church or social club. If none of these apply to you, do it for someone else's.
2. Make a game in Python or JavaScript for you to play and share with your friends.

3. Write a command-line Python script to automate something that you often have to do manually.
4. Make an app for your iOS or Android smartphone for your company, so generate market excitement and attract customers.
5. Write a PHP script to store email addresses in a MySQL database which users enter on a website. You could use this for a family newsletter, wedding invitation website or an organisation's marketing campaign.
6. Write a HTML and CSS website for a friend who sells homemade artwork, bakery, knitwear, embroidery or jewellery, and put pictures of their products on it.
7. Get in touch with a local plumber, pub or cafe with an unattractive or difficult to use website and offer to redesign it for them free of charge.
8. Make it a family project and ask your kids, spouse or parents to make something with you.

The satisfaction of creating something from nothing with your own fingers using code is hugely rewarding and one that, if you are not careful, can get addictive. The more you learn, and the more you see others using what you have made, the more rewarding it becomes and the more you will want to keep improving and keep creating better mobile, web and desktop apps.

Some of you may have been so inspired by the excitement of programming that you want to pursue a more formal line of education and I would thoroughly recommend it. Find the best school or university that you can get yourself into and soak up every iota of information that's thrown at you.

If you use your mind and commit yourself to a project, maybe you will be the person behind the next billion dollar Internet start-up or the creative genius behind an innovative lifesaving health monitoring application. It could be you who creates a web application for a new decentralised news service, or an interactive tablet application for more effectively managing personal finance. Big ideas are not hard to come by, but they are hard to make a reality. If nothing else, learn to use programming as a tool to help you make a difference in the world we live in and share together.

Afterword

Thank you for reading my book. You have spent a good deal of time working through it, and I hope that in return, you've gained a good deal of insight into the basic ideas behind computer programming.

I hope that one day I will have the privilege of meeting you and hearing how you have enjoyed reading my book. Keep me informed about what you are learning and creating. Never stop using what you learn to build applications which improve the lives of those in your local community and around the world.

Tom Bell

t.bell@hotmail.co.uk

www.codingforbeginners.co.uk

Appendix A

Python Development Environment

In order to write and execute programs we need to setup our Python interpreter and development environment. The purpose of the interpreter has been explained in Chapter 1, and it allows the code we write in Python to be understood by the computer by translating it into machine code. A *development environment* is the phrase used to refer to the program we use in order to write our code.

For simplicity, we will use the development environment which is provided along with our Python interpreter, such that when we install our interpreter we will already have our development environment setup too.

Installing the Python Interpreter

Python is open-source, meaning it is free to use and can be used in any way the user wishes. Follow these steps in order to get your Python interpreter and development environment up and running:

1. Using your browser (Google Chrome, Firefox, Safari or IE), navigate to http://www.python.org/download. Near the top of the

page you will see download links for Python 3.4.* and Python 2.7.8 (* will be the most recent version of Python whenever you view this page).

2. I recommend downloading Python 3.4.* since it is the most recent version and you should become familiar with it. You may find that there are compatibility problems with Python code you find online and this version, but in general legacy code will work in Python 3.4. Click on the download link and navigate to the bottom of the page where you will find a table of download links. Click the link that corresponds to your computer type (i.e. Windows or Mac OS X) and download it.
3. Find the location of the installer you have just downloaded and double click it to run it. Here you may have to click 'Run' or 'Yes' to confirm that you are giving the installer permission to run.
4. Once the setup wizard has launched, you should click 'Next' for every option, unless you have specific reasons not to.

Using the Python Shell

Your Python interpreter should now be installed. We'll briefly run through the operation of the Python Shell and IDLE (our development environment) and verify that the interpreter has been successfully installed.

As noted, the program that we will be using to run Python is called IDLE. If you're using a Mac, IDLE should be located in your Applications folder. On Windows, it will be accessible from the Start menu in a folder named 'Python 3.4.*'.

When you first open IDLE, you'll be presented with the Python Shell as shown below.

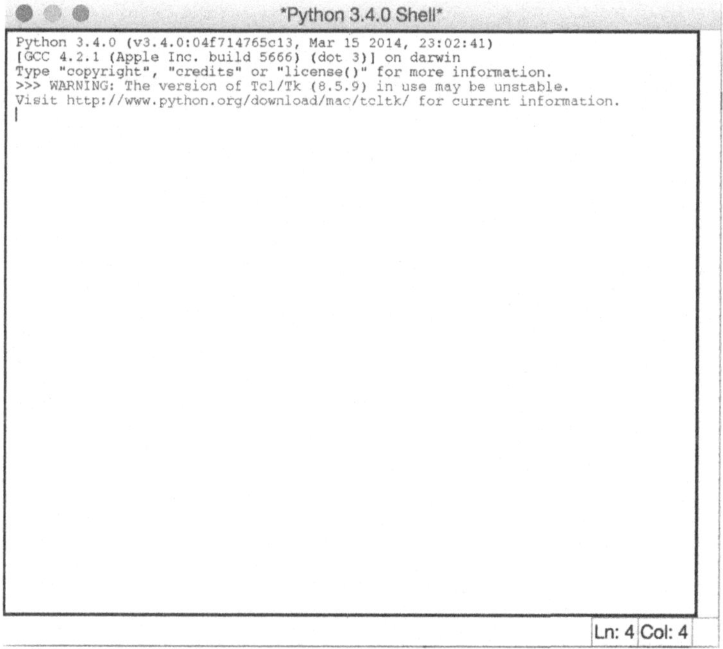

This is used to execute Python commands straight away, line-by-line. The following demonstrates its use with short sequences of mathematical calculations:

```
>>> 2+3*(4-1)
11
```

Using the IDLE Text Editor

For the majority of programming needs, it will be most appropriate not to run programs line-by-line using the Python Shell, but to create a complete document containing all of your Python source code. IDLE comes with a text editor, which you should already have installed.

From within IDLE, go to the File menu and click on 'New Window'. You should be presented with a blank document as shown below.

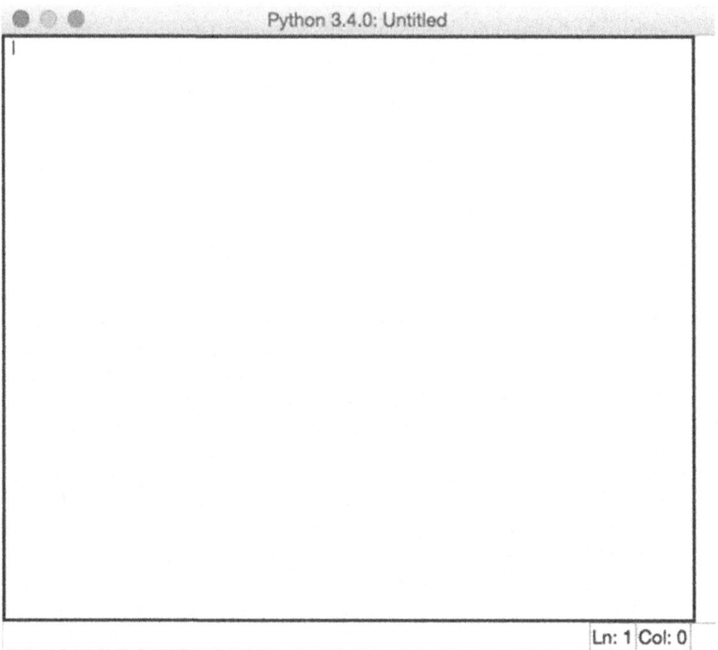

This is where you can write your own Python programs. You'll need to save this file before running it, and ensure that the file name you have chosen ends with '.py' so that your computer knows it is a Python program.

From here you can run any code from this book by simply copying what you see into the text editor and saving it. In order to run your program, simply go to the Run menu and press 'Run Module'. The output will appear in the Python Shell.

Common Programming Terms

* **(asterisk)**: A common symbol used in programming languages for multiplication.

\ **(backward slash)**: A common symbol used in programming languages for division.

— **(dash)**: A common symbol used in programming languages for subtraction.

/ **(forward slash)**: A common symbol used in programming languages for division.

Algorithm: A sequence of instructions in the form of pseudo-code or code which is used to solve a computational problem.

Array: A data type used in many programming languages as an ordered collection of data which can be accessed by specifying the element of the array that is required. They are similar to the list data type used in Python.

Artificial Intelligence (AI): A popular and important aspect of computer science which seeks to imitate and replicate the intelligence of human beings using computers in order to solve complex computational problems.

Big data: An important and powerful concept in computer science which understands the power of analysing huge databases in order to extract high-level meaningful statistics.

Boolean data type: A common data type used in many programming languages which can have the value True or False. Conditional expressions are typically evaluated to be a Boolean and are used in conditional statements such as the 'if' statement in Python.

Bug: An error in a program which causes it to function incorrectly. Bugs may be difficult to find as they may only become apparent when a program is in a very rare state. They are also often difficult to remove.

C: A popular functional programming language which uses the curly bracket syntax.

C++: An object-oriented general purpose programming language which uses curly bracket syntax. It has a similar syntax to the C programming language, but with object-oriented features.

C#: A popular object-oriented language developed by Microsoft as part of the .NET collection of languages. It is a popular language for Windows development and development on Windows smart phones.

Class: The definition of an object which acts as a template, specifying the variables and methods that an object has.

Code: An abbreviation of source code.

Comment: A line or block of text in a source code file which is used to explain the operation of parts of a program. Comments are ignored by an interpreter or compiler and are used only by developers for clarifying or describing a section of code. They are also often used to produce titles or 'read me' content at the top of a source code file.

Compiler: A program which turns the source code of a program written in a compiled language, such as C or C#, into machine code which can be directly executed on a computers CPU.

Constant: A prefix to a data type in many programming languages which specifies that the variables value cannot be changed.

Cross-platform: A term used to describe a property which some programs have to be compiled and executed on multiple operating systems.

CSS: Cascading Style Sheet. A format for specifying the stylistic features and formatting of parts of a HTML web page according to the tags, classes and id attributes used in the affected HTML elements.

Data type: A term used to describe the kind of data being stored as a variable in a programming language. Examples include integers, strings, lists and Booleans.

Debug: An activity employed by programmers which seeks to remove unwanted bugs from a program.

Editor: Also known as a text editor. A program used on a computer to create and edit the contents of a source code file. Many text editors provide additional features, such as syntax highlighting and built-in consoles.

Executable file: A file which contains the machine code of a program that has already been compiled.

For loop: A feature of many programming languages which allows a block of code to be executed a set number of times. They can be used to iterate over elements of a list any implement loops in custom algorithms.

Function: A subprogram within a program which performs a specific task within a computational system. Functions often accept parameters and return an output value.

GUI: A Graphical User Interface, defined in code and used to display content to the user and provide an intuitive interface through which a user can interact with a program.

HTML: HyperText Markup Language. A mark-up language used primarily in website which specifies the locations of content within a web page.

if statement: A feature in many programming languages which allows different blocks of code to be executed under different condition.

Infinite loop: A situation in which a loop in a program, such as a 'for' loop or a 'while' loop is unable to exit because the condition required for it to finish can never be met. An example is a 'while' loop in which the condition of the loop always evaluates to True.

Inheritance: A feature in many object-oriented programming languages which allows a class to use all of the variables and methods predefined in the class being inherited from in order to simplify the design of similar classes.

Input: A finite set of variables which are given to a program, or method at the moment they are called. Inputted data is typically processed and forms the basis of some kind of output.

Integer: A numerical data type used in many programming languages which can store positive and negative numbers with no decimal place.

Java: A common object-oriented general purpose programming language used on some websites, desktop applications and Android applications. It is very similar to C# and C++ in its syntax.

JavaScript: A web scripting language used in front-end web pages to handle user interaction with a web page and also to manage animations and other graphical effects.

Linux: A popular open source operating system used primarily by programmers, scientists and in embedded systems.

Machine code: A collection of binary instructions which have been compiled so as to be able to be understood by a CPU and executed in order to perform some computational operation.

Method: A subprogram within a class or object which performs some kind of data on the instance variables of that object and typically model some kind of real world behaviour.

Object-oriented programming: A programming paradigm in which a programming language represents the idea of objects which model a real world object or system and contain data about the object as well as methods which act upon that data.

Output: A finite set of variables that are returned from a program or method, or are displayed to a user which have some kind of meaning. Outputs are often the result of some kind of computation on input data.

Open source: An initiative which seeks to provide high quality programs, libraries and frameworks to developers for free and without restrictions on their use in order to maximise the productivity of programmers and their speed of development.

Operating system: A complex program which is executed when a computational device is turned on and provides a stable environment in which additional programs can be developed and executed more easily. Operating systems often provide features such as multi-threading, synchronisation, resource management, network management, security and power management.

PageRank: An algorithm developed by Google in order to score web pages according to their relevancy. A page's score is based not only on the number of websites which point to it, but also on the score of those websites pointing to it.

Parameter: A variable which is passed into a function of method when it is called. Also known as an '*argument*'.

Parameter list: A list defining the data types and variable names of parameters that are accepted by a function or method.

Perl: A popular interpreted programming language used primarily in web applications.

PHP: A server-side interpreted scripting language used primarily with web applications to handle user requests and to provide interaction with databases and other server-side resources.

Python: A popular programming language used primarily in web applications.

Socket: A protocol for providing low-level bidirectional communication between a client and server over a network.

Sorting: A computational task of arranging sets of variable in some kind of order as required, such as alphabetical order or numerical order. A range of algorithms exist for providing this functionality each with varying degrees of computational efficiency.

Source code: A term used to describe the contents of the file containing a complete description of a program written in a programming language.

String: A data type which stores a sequence of characters.

SQL: Structured Query Language. A querying language used to query relational databases in order to create, read, update and delete data.

User interface: A term used to describe a graphical interface provided by a program which allows users to view data and interact with it.

Variable: A packet of data stored in a program which holds data important to the operation of a program. Variables can be changed during the execution of a program.

While loop: A feature of many programming languages which enables a block of code to be executed repeatedly while a certain condition is true. Once the condition becomes false, the loop stops repeating.

Windows: A popular operating system developed by the Microsoft Corporation and used in homes and offices around the world for storing, processing and displaying content to its users.

Index